HOW TO BE A
CIVIL SERVANT

HOW TO BE A
CIVIL SERVANT

Martin Stanley

Biteback Publishing

This edition published in Great Britain in 2016 by
Biteback Publishing Ltd
Westminster Tower
3 Albert Embankment
London SE1 7SP
Copyright © Martin Stanley 2016
First published in Great Britain in 2000 by Politico's Publishing

ISBN 978-1-84954-982-0

10 9 8 7 6 5 4 3 2 1

A CIP catalogue record for this book is available from the British Library.

Set in Quadraat by Adrian McLaughlin

Printed and bound in Great Britain by
CPI Group (UK) Ltd, Croydon CR0 4YY

MIX
Paper from
responsible sources
FSC® C020471
FSC
www.fsc.org

Contents

Introduction

ORKING IN WHITEHALL can be great
fun, and very rewarding. It is good to work
to improve the lives of fellow citizens, you
get to influence important decisions, and
you get to meet some fascinating people, a good number of
them within the civil service. But new arrivals soon discover
that they are subject to a bewildering mixture of rules and procedures whilst at the same time they find it very difficult to
obtain basic advice about how to do their job. Even their more
experienced colleagues will find themselves constantly needing
to learn new skills as they move to exciting new jobs, whether
dealing with ministers for the first time or becoming involved
in a major project. And many of us need to develop leadership
and management expertise as we are given new responsibilities.

This book and its accompanying website (www.civilservant.org.uk) address these challenges by providing a thorough introduction to the duties, responsibilities and working practices of Whitehall officials. It begins by examining civil servants' professional skills, including the best way to work with ministers and in Europe. It then describes the professional and ethical constraints within which civil servants must work, including judicial review and so on. Finally, it gives advice on how to get things done in Whitehall, and in particular how to overcome obstacles to innovation, as well as describing key leadership and management skills.

I hope that the book will be found helpful by those wishing to understand the British civil service, as well as those embarking on, or facing new challenges in, their civil service career.

Martin Stanley
January 2016

Chapter 1

Working with Ministers

C IVIL SERVANTS ARE not employed to 'make policy', or 'to manage'. We are employed to achieve change on behalf of ministers. We need to make sure that every piece of advice, every brief, every management decision, every letter and every meeting takes us a little closer to our minister's objectives. One fundamental skill, therefore, is to establish a productive relationship with ministers so that we can help them achieve their long-term goals.

The Three Key Professional Duties

It is vital, when working with ministers, to recognise that we have three distinct professional duties. We need to be clear which duty we are carrying out at any one time, for each requires different skills and behaviour. Be aware that it is unlikely that you, or any other single individual, will perform really well in all three areas. Be proactive, therefore, in adding additional skills and experience to your team.

Our three duties are as follows:

1. Civil servants give advice to ministers before they make policy decisions. We must give them private, honest, informed advice and we are expected to face them with the truth even when it turns up in an inconvenient form. The Civil Service Code says that the constitutional and practical role of the civil service is to assist the government of the day with integrity, honesty, impartiality and objectivity. Put another way, we are employed to 'speak truth unto power'.

2. We must help ministers promote and defend their decisions, even if we advised against them. We must, when operating in this mode, now pay much more attention to the tone and impact of what ministers say and do, rather than focusing on the detail that underlies the policy decision. It matters little whether we think ministers are right or wrong. It is vital that their programmes are professionally promoted and defended if they are to achieve their objectives.

3. We are responsible for delivery: implementing ministers' decisions on the ground and possibly drafting the necessary

legislation. Again, we become less analytical and much more proactive. We now focus almost exclusively on ensuring the delivery of worthwhile outcomes, working closely with delivery partners both inside and outside our department. Indeed, although we undoubtedly continue to work *for* ministers, we often have to work *with* ministers in order to achieve their objectives. After all, little is as effective in driving forward a difficult agenda as a strong ministerial speech or a well-prepared meeting between a minister and a ministerial colleague, or a powerful interest group, or a delivery partner.

We carry out these duties whilst subject to numerous ethical and professional constraints which are described in some detail elsewhere in this book. But our key professional skill is to be innovative in achieving ministers' objectives without breaking any rules, and ideally without going on about how difficult it all is.

Before going into further detail, let's take a quick look at our clients.

Ministers

The most junior ministers are Parliamentary Under Secretaries of State, of whom there will be one in a small department and three or four in a large department. The word 'junior' is shorthand used across Whitehall, but that does not mean that they are not significant figures in their department. They do a great deal of important work, including piloting Bills through Parliament. They also carry out a wide range of representational and other duties, which means that they are always getting up early in the morning to attend events outside London, and then staying in the House until late in the evening to speak in adjournment debates. They take important decisions on individual cases and narrow issues. But they seldom get to take politically important decisions. These are reserved for their seniors.

In the second tier are Ministers of State, of whom there are, again, usually one to three in a department. These ministers are more experienced and powerful, and will handle – or assist Cabinet ministers with – the more complex and/ or politically tricky issues.

Then there are Cabinet ministers. Most of them are ministers in charge of departments, but there are others, including the Leader of the House of Lords and the Chief Whip. Very large or important departments also sometimes get a second minister in the Cabinet. The Chief Secretary, for instance (who negotiates government expenditure with his or her colleagues) is number two in the Treasury.

Cabinet ministers who are in charge of departments are usually styled 'Secretary of State', with some exceptions, for instance the Chancellor of the Exchequer. The title of the Secretary of State for the Home Department is almost always shortened to 'Home Secretary', and 'Foreign Secretary' is similarly a shortened form. These men and women are of course very powerful, but there is a pecking order within the Cabinet that varies with the political importance of the minister's department, and his or her personal clout and experience. But the Chancellor, the Home Secretary and the Foreign Secretary are always very influential, and invariably the top three posts in the pecking order, often out-ranking any Deputy Prime Minister – of which more below.

The whole structure is headed by the Prime Minister, and sometimes also a Deputy Prime Minister, an analysis of whose role and responsibilities is beyond the scope of this book. Suffice it to say that Prime Ministers have only a limited amount of political capital at their disposal, so they prefer to work through consensus, especially when dealing with senior and powerful colleagues. And as civil servants develop a natural loyalty to their departmental ministers, the result is that there is no clear pyramid of management responsibility within the civil service, which can make it difficult to handle cross-departmental issues.

Private Offices

... are a vital link in handling ministerial correspondence, organising the ministerial diary, conveying ministers' views to officials and providing ministers with information and views from their departments. They therefore play a crucial role in managing two precious commodities for ministers: information and time. They also play a key role in helping the minister understand – and ask difficult questions about – advice from the department.

It is worth investing a lot of time and effort into working

well with private offices. Putting on one side the fact that you should want to help them do their jobs, you also want them to think that you are helpful, knowledgeable, sensible and flexible. This is because they will communicate their views to the minister in all sorts of subtle ways – and sometimes not so subtle if they really do detest you.

The minister in charge of the department will have quite a large office – maybe twelve or more staff in a large department – headed by a Principal Private Secretary (PPS) – not to be confused with the Parliamentary Private Secretary (see below). He or she will be a more experienced official, able to act as interlocutor and trouble-shooter with senior departmental officials. The PPS is a handy first point of call if you need urgent help or advice and do not know who else to approach. PPSs are on call twenty-four hours a day, 365 days a year, and know where all the bodies are buried. For this reason, they are usually promoted when they leave private office, myself included.

A number of departments have recently created extended ministerial offices that bring together the traditional private offices, special advisers and external appointees to provide a much wider range of support functions. This should create more powerful teams around Secretaries of State, although care will need to be taken to ensure that this benefit does not accrue at the cost of less effective communication between them and their colleagues elsewhere in government, as well as within their departments, including with their junior ministers.

The officials in charge of the more junior ministers' offices are known as private secretaries (PSs) and they are usually quite

young, partly because much of the work is essentially straightforward – preparing notes of meetings and so on – and partly
because the job offers excellent experience for future senior
officials. And although the work is straightforward, that does
not mean that it is easy. The private secretary has to take a mass
of information and paperwork from the department and prepare it so that it is easy for the minister to assimilate it even in
the small hours of the morning. The private secretary might
therefore highlight certain text, or prepare a summary of a long
document, but must not distort the message when doing so.

The same applies when the private secretary is communicating the minister's views to the department, including when
preparing a note of a meeting. It is permissible to emphasise
particular points and stress any action needed, but it is not
permissible to misrepresent, distort or exaggerate the views
of the minister or anyone else. The main exception is that private secretaries will generally ignore what lawyers call *obiter
dicta*, i.e. things that are said when ministers, like the rest of
us, choose to air their views on a wide range of subjects in
the middle of a conversation about a scarcely related subject.
These comments can usually safely be ignored – but only if the
private secretary is sure that the minister will not, two weeks
later, ask what has happened about his decision to relocate a
large part of the department to his constituency.

Don't hesitate, by the way, to challenge the accuracy of a
note of a meeting, whether prepared by a private secretary or
someone in the Cabinet Secretariat. An anonymous secretary is said to have admitted to 'racking his brains to record

and report, what he thinks that they think that they ought to have thought'. The result of such a process can easily be wrong, and such meeting notes are usually too important to go uncorrected.

Things can get difficult when the minister gets angry, because the private secretary is then the one who has to transmit that anger to his or her colleagues in the department. They will usually seek to tone down the minister's comments but they, like the minister, will run out of patience if officials seem to be ignoring comments and requests. The result is that they will then quote the minister's actual words. I once saw a minute that said the Secretary of State had commented:

> This paper might well have earned reasonable marks in a university degree exam but it would score much less well in the school of life … I want the real world spelt out … As I asked for this well over a year ago … if I do not get a [revised] paper … within a month I shall commission it outside the Department.

If you get something like this then you really are in trouble.

Be aware, however, that some private secretaries get ideas well above their station. It can be very helpful if they ask 'idiot boy' questions that might well occur to someone not closely involved in your area, and they can sometimes be helpful in spotting silly mistakes, or by drawing attention to some development or ministerial view of which you were not aware. Sometimes, however, and sometimes encouraged by their ministers, they start acting as alternate policy advisers, commenting freely on the merits of your work. Watch out for this, for something has gone badly wrong if a minister prefers to hear the advice of his private secretary to that of the responsible official.

Private secretaries also control official attendance at ministers' meetings. Ideally, the minister will allow four types of official to attend. The first will be the lead official(s) responsible for preparing the advice and implementing any decisions. The second will be those, such as more senior officials and lawyers, who will provide further useful contributions to the discussion. The third, occasional attendees, will be inexperienced officials who are gaining experience of working with ministers. They are expected to keep their mouths shut and can be usefully employed in writing the note of the meeting, thus removing a chore from the private secretary. The fourth are press officers, who should be involved in discussing any issue that has a presentational aspect.

In practice, all ministers get understandably jumpy if too many officials turn up – and it also looks inefficient, especially in meetings with outsiders. The basic rule, therefore, is only one official (not counting the private secretary or special adviser) to each visitor, although you can usually get away with two officials if there is only one visitor. If there are no visitors then each minister will have their own threshold, which will be communicated to you by the private secretary. It can be particularly difficult if the minister has favourite civil servants and won't see anyone else, even if someone else knows much more about the subject under discussion. But you have to accept the minister's decision and there is no point in shouting at the poor private secretary, who probably hates it as much as you do.

The daily life of a private office revolves around 'the box' – the red, rectangular box in which the minister carries his or her homework. Some ministers, to everyone's amazement, manage to sign all their letters and respond to all their submissions when in the office. Others take several boxes home each night and then never touch them. But most plough through one or two boxes, if only because they contain some quite fascinating stuff.

A typical box will contain a red 'immediate' folder of items requiring urgent decision or action, about which the private secretary will ask first thing in the morning. Then there will be a diary folder, prepared by the Diary Secretary – a position that can be one of the worst jobs in Whitehall. There are no thanks if everything goes well, but immediate retribution if something goes wrong: 'How could you send me to Wigan North Western when I should have gone to Wigan Wallgate? Didn't you [a nineteen-year-old who has never been north of Wembley Arena] know the difference?' Ministers also accuse novice diary secretaries of arranging meetings to which the minister had not agreed, and so on. They quickly learn never to confirm any engagement without the minister's signature, preferably in blood.

Diary secretaries will therefore threaten to maim any official who has the temerity to tell a member of the public that the minister's diary is free at a certain time. This is because the member of the public will then expect to be able to arrange a meeting at that time and, if the meeting is not then arranged, they will know that the minister chose not to see them, rather than that the minister was literally unable to see them. Frequently, therefore, you will be trapped between a member of the public (who cannot understand why it takes more than thirty seconds to check that the minister is free – have we never heard of telephones and computers?) and the diary secretary (who will ensure that nothing in your official life will ever run sweetly again if you dare to commit the minister without his or her written agreement – which will not be forthcoming for several weeks). What is the best way of handling this problem? I wish I knew.

The rest of the box will contain folders full of submissions, letters for signature, and background information. Christopher Jary reckons that a typical Secretary of State's red box may include:

- Twenty-five letters to sign;

- Fifteen submissions;

- Ten draft replies to Parliamentary Questions (PQs);

- Five invitations to consider;

- Two draft press releases;

- One draft speech to approve;

- One Q&A brief;

- One parliamentary statement to approve;

- 110 press cuttings;

- Twenty briefings;

- Fifteen letters from Cabinet colleagues;

- Eight papers and attachments for tomorrow;

- A folder of papers from special advisers.

Some of the papers that do not require a decision may not get read (would you read them at one o'clock in the morning?). And the 'papers for tomorrow' may get put on one side to be looked at just before – or in the car on the way to – the meeting. The letters get signed, if they look sensible, often without the minister looking at the covering note from officials. So, if the minister should definitely give some thought to whether he really wants to sign the letter, you must get the private secretary to put a big red note on top.

Officials' formal advice to ministers is contained in 'submissions' which will also get looked at in varying depth, depending upon how sensible the recommendation – at the top of the document – seems to appear. Again, therefore, do not hide a little bombshell in the middle of a submission. You may think that you are protecting your back, but this ploy will cut no ice with the minister when the unexpected bomb detonates a day or two later. It is also worth noting that private secretaries may be tempted to edit a long badly structured submission, and this can be dangerous if the PS doesn't know the policy area very well. This is one of the reasons why short, clear submissions are to be preferred.

Paper is of course often giving way to electronics in the form of BlackBerrys, tablets and mobile phones, speeding communication but also adding somewhat to the complexity of organising a ministerial life.

By the way, don't be surprised or upset if you hear that an incoming minister has 'sacked' the private secretary they have inherited from their predecessor. It is vital that there is good personal chemistry between the minister and his or her PS, and the absence of such chemistry does not imply any fault on either side. I used to advise ministers to consider whether they would be happy to sit next to a candidate PS during a very long flight. Foreign Secretary Douglas Hurd had a second test.

You are sitting at the top table at a public dinner. The far door of the hotel ballroom opens and your private secretary appears clutching a piece of paper. It will not simply say that the PM has altered the time of your meeting tomorrow, because that would not justify the interruption. It will carry some news, almost certainly bad.

Will you look forward to sharing your first reaction to that news with the individual now crossing the floor towards you? If the candidate looks like failing this test, then no amount of intellectual or professional qualifications will make up for the deficiency.

Ministerial Aides

One or two other interesting species can be found in and around private offices.

All ministerial departments have one or more **special advisers** (often abbreviated to 'spads' or 'Spads') who are personal appointees of the Secretary of State but employed as temporary civil servants. They are a valuable addition to the minister's team, for three main reasons.

The first and obvious reason is that it gives ministers immediate and simultaneous access to a friendly and familiar face offering political advice to be considered alongside that from mainstream civil servants. It is not surprising that many ministers prefer to have near them devils that they know rather than devils they don't – especially at the beginning of their time in government. They have chosen them (rather than had them imposed upon them) unlike their civil servants and often their departmental junior ministers – and they are likely to have compatible personalities.

The second, equally obvious, reason is that spads can give strong political advice, help draft political speeches etc., thus providing an extra pair of hands when there is ever-increasing pressure on ministerial time.

And the third, also very strong, reason is that special advisers can often provide a different perspective – a counterpoint, if you will – to the advice emanating from the official machine. Officials' recommendations may require ministers to take unacceptable political risks – or indeed operational and financial risks. (The National Audit Office has examined many policy decisions over the years and does not believe that the generality of civil servants are risk averse. Rather, it believes that officials too often do not understand the risks that are associated with what they want to do.) Conversely, officials' advice may be too cautious and/or reflect a certain inertia carried over from the policies of a different minister – including a different minister within the same party. As one spad put it:

> The last thing any Secretary of State needs is another civil servant. They've got enough of them and that's not really meant as a criticism, it is just you inevitably inherit a policy inertia ... You were eyes and ears for policy going awry and also the eyes and ears for policy initiatives that you've inherited perfectly innocently that of course are now contrary to government policy or government intent. We were a third party, a devil's advocate.

Spads' duties may be summarised as follows:

- They are exempt from mainstream civil servants' obligation of political impartiality;

- They can assist ministers on any aspect of departmental business;

- They can convey ministers' views, instructions and priorities to officials;

- They can ask officials to prepare and provide information and data, including internal analyses and papers; and

- They are allowed to engage in limited political activities outside the office, such as telephone canvassing.

But...

- They cannot engage in public canvassing such as for parliamentary candidates in constituencies;

- They cannot line manage regular civil servants;

- Nor may officials' advice be transmitted to ministers via special advisers;

- And spads may not formally represent the government or their minister, not commit the government in any way.

There are also a number of spads in No. 10, subject to the same constraints.

Within the broad job description summarised above, the role, experience and abilities of spads vary a great deal. Some focus on policy issues and some on the media. As they are directly appointed by the Secretary of State, they can sometimes have even greater influence than departmental ministers.

One or two can be difficult to work with, but the vast majority are generally helpful and keen to work with officials. You should work co-operatively with them, respecting their different but complementary experience and responsibilities. You must keep in close touch with them on issues that are likely to attract their attention, and you should be ready with advice and information.

> As an adviser, the first time you meet with a senior manager in the public service, they are going to think that you got your job because of your politics ... and that they are there because of their superior knowledge, skill, ability and performance. Neither is necessarily true, but that is often the starting point from which a partnership has to be built, a partnership that needs to be characterised by robust discussion, understanding of each other's roles and respectful conduct.
>
> —MARK MADDEN

Although special advisers may attend meetings with outside organisations, and sometimes make speeches on behalf of their ministers, they do not represent the government in any formal sense.

They may let you know their minister's views and work priorities, and may, on behalf of their minister, ask you to do work of a fact-finding or advisory nature. They cannot give you instructions on their own behalf, although they can pass on instructions from ministers. If you are concerned that the spad may have misinterpreted a minister's instruction, or if you feel that the minister's decision needs to be challenged for some reason, you should contact one of the private secretaries.

Your advice to ministers should always be communicated via private offices, even if previously seen in draft by a special adviser. If they wish to comment on your advice, they should do so in a separate minute.

Like private secretaries, special advisers can be an excellent source of advice about ministers' policy instincts and priorities. It is certainly worth talking to them before putting up any major submission, and it is usually a good idea to give them a chance to comment on your draft. However, do not make the mistake of letting a special adviser steer you in a direction that seems unwise. Maybe the special adviser's advice will be different to yours, and maybe the Secretary of State will not take your advice, and maybe the special adviser will accurately foretell the Secretary of State's decision, but that should not stop you putting up advice in which you believe.

One difference between permanent civil servants and special advisers is that the latter are usually fiercely loyal to their minister, on whose career they themselves depend, and sensitive to what they perceive as disloyal criticism. For instance, it is quite OK to ask a private secretary what on earth caused the minister to say such and such a thing to a visitor. The private secretary will explain what went wrong, or acknowledge that the minister made a mistake, and then you can get on and loyally sort out the resultant problem. But if you put the same question to a special adviser, they will often go into defensive mode or, even worse, tell the minister what you said, which hardly helps build up a long-term relationship. So it is best to give spads the clear impression that you believe that their minister walks on water. They will suspect that you are lying, but respect you for it.

You should also watch out for demarcation disputes with special advisers. Many ministers thrive on a steady diet of witty or barnstorming speeches, which civil servants are not equipped to provide. And although we should stand ready to rebut factually incorrect stories, we are not equipped to provide a political reputation management service that swings into action whenever the minister is criticised in the media. Both of these tasks should properly fall to special advisers, but they are often under enormous pressure and cannot see why they should not get help from the massed ranks of the department. There is usually nothing for it but to stick to your guns. You must certainly never, ever start writing political speeches. But holding the line is much easier if you have first established yourself as someone who is keen and highly able to help ministers achieve their objectives.

The No. 10 Policy Unit contains a mixture of special advisers and permanent civil servants. Individuals within the unit can be very influential. You should therefore work closely with the member of the unit assigned to shadow your department whenever your subject comes to their attention. Equally, however, don't automatically assume that any one individual in the unit is speaking on behalf of the unit, or on behalf of the Prime Minister. They may well be doing so, but they may also be giving their own views that may not be shared by others.

Parliamentary Private Secretaries (confusingly, also known as PPSs) are not civil servants but MPs who help senior ministers with their parliamentary duties. They often attend meetings within the department and should be given as much help and information as possible. However, their duties are primarily party political and they hold no formal office on behalf of the voter or taxpayer. There are therefore obvious limits to the amount of assistance that they can be given by officials and they should only be given otherwise confidential information if it is clearly necessary for the discharge of their parliamentary and political duties.

Parliamentary clerks look after departments' relations with Parliament, ensuring that questions are answered, Bill amendments laid and so on. They are usually both very knowledgeable and helpful. Indeed, they like to be asked questions because it greatly helps them if you understand their systems and timescales.

Information officers work in the press office but usually develop a very close working relationship with ministers, and so should form a key part of your extended team. They will help you design media strategies, draft press releases etc. and they will oversee any contact with journalists. Involve them very early on, as you need to 'design in' the way in which you will explain and communicate any new policy. However, like you, they will not seek to 'spin' a story in the sense of seeking to leave a journalist with an over-favourable impression of a development. New ministers and special advisers therefore frequently compare them unfavourably with party press officers, although the more experienced ones come to admire the trust that can be built up between specialist reporters and their departmental opposite numbers.

Ministers' Duties

Ministers owe certain important duties to their civil servants.

First, they must consider your advice, even if they do not take it. They cannot tell you what to do without first giving you an opportunity to advise them on the suitability of their proposed course of action. The Ministerial Code says that 'ministers have a duty to give fair consideration and due weight to informed and impartial advice from civil servants...'

On the other hand, ministers are, to some extent, free to choose how they will receive your advice. Some will have meetings only with selected officials. If you are not in that group then you will always have to submit advice on paper. Other ministers hate paper, and you will need to be able to brief them – succinctly but effectively – in meetings or in the back of the ministerial car. But note that ministers may not require you to give them advice in public or in front of a TV camera, and the advice that you give to ministers will not normally be made public. It can be difficult enough to give contentious advice whilst worrying about the reactions of your colleagues. It is twice as difficult if you also have to take account of the possible reaction of outside observers, journalists or television viewers. Equally, it is important that ministers should be allowed to reject your advice without fearing criticism for having done so.

Note also that, if the decision is important, you must prepare, and the minister must have the opportunity to read, a written submission, although it often makes sense for this to be followed by a meeting – and if you think that such a discussion would be helpful then you should ask for one. I must stress, however, that important decisions must never be based merely on oral briefing or a PowerPoint presentation. This is to ensure that the decision is soundly based on a proper consideration of all the relevant facts and arguments. The aim is to develop evidence-based policy, not policy-based evidence.

For instance, a minister pleased with the apparent success of a programme might encourage his or her officials to think about an encore. Such encouragement can appear welcome, but must be resisted until the case for and against the further programme has been properly thought through. And there is a less positive reason. A formal submission is a defence against a minister who might not accept advice and then subsequently seeks to blame his or her officials.

If a minister makes a decision that you consider to be seriously wrong then you have the right – indeed, it is your responsibility – to check (a) that the minister has been presented in writing with all the relevant facts and arguments, and with a clear recommendation, in a form which he or she can easily assimilate, and (b) that he or she has understood all the important factors. If this has not happened then you should consult the minister's private secretary about the best way to correct matters.

Further written advice will often be enough, including any

necessary apology for failing to prepare comprehensive advice the first time round. But if comprehensive advice has already been submitted, and the decision is important enough, then you should press for the opportunity to argue the case a second time, preferably in person. If the minister still rejects your recommendation then you must accept the decision. It is not for you to question the political or strategic thinking that might have contributed to the decision in question unless, exceptionally, the minister appears to be ignoring legal advice or defying government policy, e.g. by failing to consult interested colleagues.

Second, ministers may not ask you to help them circumvent collective discussion, e.g. by announcing a 'decision' whilst a ministerial colleague remains opposed to it. If you are caught in such cross-fire you should either refer the issue to your Permanent Secretary or seek collective resolution by involving the Cabinet Secretariat, who will arrange discussions at the necessary level.

Third, ministers may not ask you to do things that are illegal or improper. For instance, they may not ask you to pay a subsidy (a 'state aid') that is prohibited under European law. And they may not tell you to commit expenditure unless you have obtained the necessary approvals, e.g. from the Treasury. It is not enough for your minister to assure you that he has spoken to the Chief Secretary and received the OK. The Chief Secretary may have a quite different recollection of the same conversation, or at the very least has a duty to consult his or her civil servants before making the decision.

Fourth, ministers may not ask you to hide things from interested officials and ministers in your own or other departments. It is of course sometimes sensible to work up a proposal before showing it to colleagues. After all, although you do not work only for your own ministers, you certainly work first for your ministers. But you may not collude in a 'bounce' and if you feel that colleagues in another department would expect to be told about a proposal, then you must tell them – and you should ensure that your ministers are equally well informed. It is embarrassing, to say the least, if they find that the Chief Secretary appears to know more than they do.

The main exception to this rule is that there is no need for you to disclose your own and your minister's negotiating position in a public expenditure negotiation. But the relevant facts which underlie your position must be disclosed.

Fifth, ministers should be polite to their officials – because of course we cannot answer back. In practice, we can forgive an occasional flash of bad temper, recognising that ministers are often under great pressure. Indeed, it is worth remembering the rule of thumb that ministers who are constantly charming in public are often (not always) less than considerate to their staff (and vice versa). I suspect that that is because we all have only a limited amount of charm to hand around. And ministers are human, too, with the usual run of human strengths and weaknesses. But consistent bullying, rudeness and foul language are unacceptable, not least because they damage the minister him- or herself. Bullies are avoided and not told things. They are placated and not served.

It can be hard to know what to do if a minister appears to be breaching one of the above rules. If you know the minister well enough, and if you are sure that you are not being thin-skinned, you should raise any concerns yourself. Alternatively you might consult the minister's private secretary. And failing that you should enlist the help of a senior colleague.

Giving Advice to Ministers

Ministers vary greatly in the way in which they work with their ministerial colleagues, the public, the media and their officials. The best civil servants are therefore very good at putting themselves in their ministers' shoes, and understanding their fears, ambitions and pressures. We understand that ministers are employed on precarious short-term contracts, and are constantly trying to balance a number of conflicting pressures. Ministers need to know that civil servants understand those pressures. If this does not come naturally, then set some time aside to reflect on why a minister took that unexpected decision, or said or wrote that unexpected thing. There is always a reason, even if you would not always agree that it is a good one.

We have a professional duty to give clear, unbiased advice, based on a sound knowledge of the facts and a wise analysis of the competing arguments. Above all, we understand the need to question both explicit and implicit assumptions, especially those about human, corporate or national economic behaviour. We make full use of our common sense or instincts, drawing on our experience in the policy area in question. And above all we give advice that will deliver worthwhile outcomes, not just in some idealised Whitehall world but in real schools, hospitals or barracks.

The best civil servants also know that their advice will often be unwelcome or unexpected, so they do not expect it to be accepted straight away. There is usually a moment to be seized, but you might have to wait for it.

Indeed, you should never tell a minister that he or she cannot do something unless you also offer them an alternative approach which substantially achieves the same political objective, or at the very least undertake to look for a way round the obstacle, and to report back very quickly. You must therefore develop the ability to distinguish between ministers' fundamental objectives and the specific solutions that they might put forward, which might not be workable or affordable.

Remember, too, that, as ministers are under constant pressure, you must do everything possible to help them work quickly, efficiently and effectively. Always prepare your work in a way that allows them to concentrate on essential decisions and on presentation. Be succinct – especially in meetings. And definitely read David Laughrin's summary of ministers' needs, 'In Their Own Words'. You might also like to read David's *Political Quarterly* article on ministerial overload ('Swimming for Their Lives – Waving or Drowning?') and what should be done to tackle it. Both are on the www.civilservant.org.uk website.

Ministers are inevitably very concerned to perform well in Parliament. It is particularly important that they are well prepared for Oral Parliamentary Questions, Statements and Debates, all of which can be very testing even for experienced ministers. When discussing these with ministers, you should not assume that political opponents are also enemies. Parliament operates rather like an old-fashioned club. Fierce public debate is often for show, and political opponents are often surprisingly friendly when not on public view.

Ministers hate it when civil servants hog the thinking time. It is often the case that we know that a difficult decision needs to be taken in, for example, five days' time. We then spend four (or four and a half) days crafting elegant advice. This cannot possibly allow the minister enough time to reflect on the issue, let alone ask for further information or consultations. Of course it will take you some time to consult colleagues, consider all the options etc. But, as a rule of thumb, you should put up a preliminary submission, if only for information, about half way through your thinking period. If nothing else, this will give the minister a chance to reflect on the issue in bed at night. And he or she will be able to feed in their own thoughts and questions before it is too late. We may not welcome substantial changes to our proposals – but it is better to know about them before the deadline is only a few hours away.

Similarly, ministers hate surprises. They need to be told bad news, told about serious problems, and told when important decisions are brewing, as soon as you are aware of them.

They may not be very pleased, but they will be a lot less pleased if they first hear of the problem from someone else, or even worse from the press, and then find out that you knew all along.

Remember, too, that ministerial thinking time needs to be built into the diary, but often isn't. If you get to work in a private office, try to build in a number of quiet slots and strategy discussions.

There is of course a lot more to persuading a minister than simply providing logical advice. As noted above, your advice is much more likely to be accepted if you have already established that you understand political realities. A special adviser once put it very well when he suggested that 'civil servants should be politically aware, not politically aligned'. More generally, you want to be perceived as a professional – such as a solicitor – who is on the side of the minister and committed to helping them do their job really well. Once you have established that relationship, it is easier to give occasional unpalatable advice.

You also need to show that you can cope with setbacks and can dig yourself – and your minister – out of a hole. Indeed, if you have made a mistake yourself, and then said sorry and done your best to put it right, you will probably find that this results in your having a stronger relationship with your minister. He or she will have made mistakes too!

More widely, however, you need to show that you understand 'the real world' outside Whitehall, and are innovative and enthusiastic. Personal impressions count heavily with ministers. They want to be able to rely on the enthusiasm and professionalism of their officials, and are very disappointed if officials do not seem committed to their objectives, or are in any way unimpressive, hesitant or over-cautious, or if they do not seem to know what they are talking about. You are paid to be creative and to look for solutions. You should make it clear that obstacles frustrate you, too. You should also tell them about your successes, and prepare very carefully for even the most routine meetings with them. This will reinforce their trust in you, and this in turn will give you greater authority in your dealings with others.

Also (I hate to say this, but it is important) remember that your clothes, appearance and body language send clear messages, whether you want them to or not. Take care that those messages are the ones that you wish to send, both to ministers and to colleagues.

Civil Servants

Now let's look at your fellow officials.

There used to be common structures and staff grades across the civil service, but these have mainly disappeared, leaving some departments using numbers (Grade 7 etc.), some using pay bands (Band A etc.) and some using descriptors (Policy Assistant, Senior Policy Adviser etc.). But as there are no common titles used across Whitehall, some of the old titles live on, including in this book. The main ones, at Grade 7 and above, are shown in the following table:

	VERY OLD TITLE	OLD TITLE	NOWADAYS OFTEN KNOWN AS
Senior	Cabinet Secretary and Head of the Civil Service		
Civil	Permanent Secretary		
Service	(Civil Service Head of Department)		
	Deputy Secretary	Grade 2	Director General
	Under Secretary	Grade 3	Director
	Assistant Secretary	Grade 5	Director or Deputy Director
	Senior Principal & Principal	Grade 6 & Grade 7	Deputy Director, Assistant Director, Team Leader, Policy Manager etc.

Internally, when talking about senior staff across Whitehall, some now find it convenient to refer to the 'pay bands' (PBs) established by the Cabinet Office, where PB1 = the old Grade 5, PB2 = Grade 3 and PB3 = Grade 2.

What do these senior people do? They help ministers and other officials deliver ministers' objectives, both by giving advice to ministers and by implementing ministers' decisions. They need to be able to work closely and effectively with ministers, with other Whitehall civil servants, with the wider civil service, with the private and voluntary sectors and with pressure groups. They operate more like a club than a hierarchical organisation, and that is simultaneously their great strength and their great weakness – a subject to which I return later.

The key grade is Grade 7. Grade 7s are expected to know all there is to know about their policy area, and to know all the key players, pressure groups and so on. In a well-run department, you will find that senior officials listen very carefully to their Grade 7s, and tend to operate in a way which supports their Grade 7s, rather than vice versa.

There are 4,000-plus staff in the senior civil service (SCS), including many who work outside Whitehall, many specialists and many who have been recruited direct from the private and voluntary sectors. SCS jobs vary hugely, but usually include one or more of the following:

- Agreeing strategic aims with ministers, and communicating those aims to Grade 7s and others;

- Agreeing and providing the financial and human resources needed to achieve those aims;

- Deploying their greater knowledge and experience in support of Grade 7s;

- Trouble-shooting;

- Undertaking complex casework and project management; and

- Acting as a personal adviser to ministers, of which more below.

The breadth of responsibilities grows wider with increasing grade, but it is seldom necessary for there to be a Grade 5 and a Grade 3 and a Grade 2 between the key Grade 7 and the Permanent Secretary/Head of Department. Most departments structure themselves so as to cut out one of these tiers (though not always the same one) in each management hierarchy.

It is worth noting that the more senior officials are not

necessarily more powerful. They have to rely on others both for information and for delivery, and they are often heavily constrained by (small p) political factors, including the independence of each Secretary of State and hence the independence of each departmental senior management team. Other constraints on senior officials include the need to avoid annoying ministers, and the club-like nature of senior officialdom. The latter can be a good thing, in that it encourages senior officials to work collaboratively rather than just for their own ministers. It also allows pay levels to be set relatively low, in return for lots of genuine job satisfaction. But the 'clubbiness' of the senior civil service can also lead to senior officials being over-tactful in their dealings with one another, which can delay change, lead to poor annual appraisals, and create confused expectations.

Chapter 2

Professional Skills

EFFECTIVE COMMUNICATION

BOTH MINISTERS AND officials live or die by our communications skills. We often have no other weapon at our disposal. But we are not communicating with machines. We are trying to achieve things by influencing the behaviour of other human beings. That means that we must first understand the **purpose** of the communication, its **content,** and its **audience** (including their beliefs), and then – if we are to strike a chord with our audience – our communications need **emotion,**

energy and **intelligence** – which means being clear, logical and accurate.

Purpose and Content

Before you turn to your keyboard, pick up a pen or turn up for a meeting, take a little time to decide:

- What you expect to the recipient to do once they have read your missive, or what action you expect to be taken following your meeting;

- When you expect it to be done; and (if appropriate)

- How much work you expect to create.

The answers to these questions are not always obvious and, if they are not obvious to you, they will certainly not be obvious to the recipient. Are you looking for a decision, information or advice? Are you seeking to persuade, and if so are you expecting confirmation that you have been successful?

It is particularly important to think about the amount of work that you are creating. You may think you are asking a simple question, but the recipient might be able to answer it at a number of levels after varying degrees of research. So do you want them to spend fifteen minutes, or fifteen hours, on the reply? This question is particularly relevant if you are addressing a request to several people. For instance, if you send out a request for briefing or information to the heads of ten divisions, and they each pass it out to four branches, and if each branch then has to do three hours' work, you have created 120 hours of work. Even more work can be created when ministers write to other ministers, and to trade associations and the heads of large organisations. Do you really intend this? Could you not target the request more carefully, or write to a sample of recipients?

Once you have answered the above three questions to your own satisfaction, you should include the result in the first few sentences of your letter or minute, or at the end of the meeting. There is no need for this to appear as an order. You can add plenty of words and phrases like 'please', 'I should be grateful if' and 'it would be helpful if'. But do not disguise your expectations. The recipient needs these to be crystal clear.

If you are simply seeking agreement to a proposal, phrase your minute in such a way that a simple 'yes' or 'no' can be given by the recipient, e.g. finish the minute: 'Do you agree, please?'

The Audience

It is obvious that an audience of subject experts will need to be approached in quite a different way to an audience with only a general interest in your subject – and that applies whether you are planning a speech or a magazine article or a letter. It is also obvious that a letter to a concerned member of the public will most likely need to be drafted in quite a different way from a letter to a colleague in the Treasury. At the very least, they will have different shared assumptions and different levels of interest in features such as the legal background to the issue.

It is also important to recognise that otherwise similar people can have quite different attitudes, responses and beliefs. Jonathan Haidt, in *The Righteous Mind: Why Good People Are Divided by Politics and Religion*, explains very clearly how different people can perceive 'fairness' in different ways, and can have different perceptions of, and attitudes to, the risk of moral hazard associated with, for instance, welfare payments. And do be aware of the voluminous research that shows that most of our deeply held beliefs and prejudices will not be altered by logical argument and hard evidence. We are strongly attached to much of what we believe and we change such views only very slowly, and in response to gentle encouragement, not aggressive debate. It is important to bear all these truths in mind both when planning communication strategies and when preparing individual communications.

One topical example might be the debate about climate change. Those concerned with its consequences have often been seen as too relaxed about forgoing economic growth, and so not being concerned about worldwide poverty, but instead being more concerned about 'a few polar bears and low-lying islands'. They have learned, I think, to focus on issues which resonate much more with doubters – such as energy security, wastefulness and affordability – and to talk about the threat to Norfolk, or even London, rather than the Marshall Islands.

And we sometimes have to deal with people who are highly stressed or obsessive or worse. Such people need to receive very clear, unambiguous information and advice, or else you will get absolutely nowhere. It is always a mistake to be rude or to show anger or frustration. Such reactions (a) raise the emotional temperature, and so get in the way of clear communication; (b) immediately make people dislike you; and (c) lay you open to criticism. All these severely reduce your effectiveness.

Emotion

We should never neglect the need for emotion and humanity when we speak and when we write, either for our own or for our minister's signature. Emotions make a very clear impression on those with whom we are communicating, and contribute greatly to the effectiveness of our communications. They should therefore form a small but vital part of almost all communications, including inter-ministerial correspondence, ministerial submissions, letters to the public and speeches – indeed, any communication in which you are trying to persuade or leave a lasting impression. Dry, official-sounding texts are simply less effective in these circumstances.

We must also always be polite and, if there is anything to apologise for – including a late reply – then apologise generously, using the word 'sorry' (as ever, a short Anglo-Saxon word is the most effective). Always try to avoid jargon, officialese, legalese, foreign or Latin phrases, acronyms and abbreviations. And please avoid insincerity. I distrust rounding-off sentences at the end of letters, e.g. 'I hope you find these comments helpful.' These words are certainly entirely inappropriate if the letter conveys unwelcome news.

Be aware, too, that words with similar meanings can carry somewhat different emotional connotations. Returning to the climate change example, I have read that some scientists wish that they had not warned about 'global warming' but instead used the much more threatening 'global overheating'.

Energy

To be effective, it is also necessary to impart some sense of motivation, commitment or direction. For instance, it is not enough to demonstrate, in a ministerial submission, that you are familiar with the facts, and are concerned about them. You also have to show that you intend to do something about the issue. Only then will a minister be happy to leave you to get on with your job.

Similarly, a minister, when writing to colleagues or the public, needs to demonstrate that he or she appreciates what is troubling the correspondent and demonstrate his or her determination to deal with the point at issue. As one Secretary of State commented:

> Many civil servants seem too concerned to flesh out all the detail that they know to pay attention to impact, logic and narrative. Correspondence, for example, needs to explain policies in plain English with good illustrative stories that connect with the experience of the

intended recipients. It needs to avoid the kind of recital of clichés or jargon that is sometimes served up.

Intelligence

Your approach to the draft will depend, of course, on whether you are still at the stage of designing your policy or whether you are implementing or defending it. But, whichever applies, it is essential that the contents are clear, logical and accurate, whether we are communicating within Whitehall or with the public. Many of our communications deal with subjects that are important either to our ministers or to sections of the public, or to both. None of us will get very far unless we learn to write accurately and unambiguously. Indeed, all experienced civil servants have real skill in this area.

The structure of written text can make all the difference, especially if the subject is a complex one. Do not hesitate to make full use of side headings. 'Background' and 'Next Steps' or 'Action' are particularly useful. Also make full use of annexes to reduce the length, and improve the flow, of the main document. If you are asking more than one question, or dealing with more than one issue, consider giving each a separate section and a separate heading. And remember that one table of figures, or one graph, can often do the job of several pages of words.

It is also essential that we properly explain the considerations that underlie ministers' policies. It is a real cop-out to use phrases such as 'It is the department's policy that...' The obvious retort is 'Why?'

Trust

Especially when dealing with ministers, attention to the above factors tends to increase their trust in you – and trust is a valuable commodity which is hard to gain and easy to lose. The latter happens, for instance, as a result of simple mistakes, failure to check statistics or consistency, and a failure to understand the political background to the issue. Remember that civil servants should be politically aware, not politically aligned.

Accuracy or Pedantry?

As I have discovered to my cost, the best way to wake up an audience of senior officials is to put up a slide that includes a misplaced apostrophe. This is not (just?) because they are a bunch of boring pedants. It is mainly because, like lawyers, they are trained to write accurately and unambiguously. Rightly or wrongly, therefore, they will write you off as unintelligent if you make grammatical and other mistakes that are commonly made by lots of other (very intelligent) people. So do make sure you know the difference between its and it's, and avoid common errors such as mixing up principle and principal. (Hint – the person has got 'pal' at the end.)

If you need help, then I recommend Graham King's *Collins Good Grammar*.

Emails, Spell-Check etc.

Emails are quick and easy to send, but surprisingly permanent and often the source of regret. They are always worth a second look for tone, content and list of recipients. Does the whole department need to read your reply? And I (almost) never blind copy an email. If it would be seriously bad for the addressee to know that you had done so, just think how they will feel when a blind copy recipient hits 'reply all'. The only exception might be when blind copying to a long circulation list of people who probably do not want their email addresses to be shown to many others. But even then there is a risk that you will one day forget to blind copy, and instead email openly to all of them. If this risk is unacceptable then you will need to use Twitter and/or a blog or other mechanism to communicate with larger numbers.

Spell-check is good, but fallible. It happily accepts minster and manger rather than minister and manager, and will allow you to forward a daft letter. And one official found himself briefing a minister on Aids in Uganda that '74 per cent of sufferers had had contact with women and 26 per cent contact with me'. If the document is important, get someone to read it who has not seen it before.

I confess that I am an obsessive hoarder of emails – assuming they can be organised in a way that makes some sort of sense. In part this is because the cost of doing so – in time or money – is so very low that it is easily repaid by the occasional value of finding that old email that proves that you had specified the correct time for the appointment, or had issued a sufficiently clear warning that a colleague was about to do something stupid. Of course it's not so good when they prove the opposite, but at least you can then issue a swift apology.

PRESENTATIONAL SKILLS

I make no apology for stressing the importance of presentation so early in this book. It is an intrinsic part of policy development, because it is never enough, in today's society, merely to introduce new laws and regulations and then expect instant obedience. We have to get the public on our side, or else even the cleverest of policies will fail. This is a particular problem if we are trying to address one of the 'wicked issues', those that affect many people – some of them strongly opinionated – but where our knowledge is incomplete and where solutions may impact on other problem areas. Indeed, some parts of Whitehall have come to recognise that they are involved in what amounts to a permanent campaign to achieve change in areas as diverse as local taxation and the consumption of dangerous drugs.

We must also remember that very few people read guidance material, however well written. New regulations therefore need to be easy to understand, and clearly communicated via the media, if they are to be generally accepted and easily enforced. The main purpose of guidance material should be to answer questions about the application of the new rules to non-standard situations.

We must therefore design policies that are easily communicated. Furthermore, presentation needs to be considered right at the beginning of the policy process, not near the end, because policies that are hard to understand, and hard to defend, are generally flawed. The time to think about this is before you choose your policy option, not right at the end of the process. White Papers, consultation documents etc. should make it crystal clear how each proposal will make life better for ordinary members of the public, for business or for other sectors.

Let's now fast forward beyond the policy design stage to the point at which ministers' decisions need to be announced, and so become the object of critical scrutiny by other politicians and the media. We now have a duty to be less analytical and instead help ministers present their policies and decisions in the best possible light. In order to carry out this task, we must put aside any doubts (and sometimes also put aside inconvenient facts) and look at the issue through ministers' eyes in order to help them express their beliefs and defend their policies as effectively as possible.

Whenever you are thinking about the presentational aspects of a policy, there are a few things to bear in mind.

- We need to be constantly on the look-out for opportunities for ministers to publicise their policies and their programmes. We need to be proactive in looking for media and other opportunities, including in connection with developments in related policy areas elsewhere in the department or Whitehall.

- Don't be mesmerised by the media. There are lots of other ways to communicate your policies, including via the web and by getting key opinion formers and senior stakeholders on your side.

- Ministers will usually want their policies to be set within the government's wider agenda. So every important speech, letter or magazine article has to speak to current key themes before focusing on its particular subject. If you do not have a note of current themes – and they do change from time to time – then consult your press office.

- Do bear in mind that there are strict limits to how far we can go without compromising our political impartiality. On the one hand, it is perfectly proper for us to prepare drafts for ministers (including draft Parliamentary Answers) that praise the government's policies, and it is perfectly proper for our drafts to omit facts and arguments that might cast doubt on the appropriateness of those policies. In doing this, we are not being unprofessional. Rather, like the barrister whose principal duty is to the court and who does not necessarily believe in the client's case, we are simply providing the best possible professional service to our clients, without going so far as to mislead either the minister or Parliament. On the other hand, we may not explicitly or implicitly criticise either the members or the policies of the opposition, nor may we criticise the actions or performance of the current opposition whilst they were in government. Also, anything in a draft that purports to be a fact must be verifiable. Nor may we serve up unverifiable generalisations. If you feel that ministers would want to make a statement which cannot be verified then you should suggest that they say something like: 'I believe it is clear that...' or something of the sort, so attributing the statement to the minister, rather than implying that it cannot be questioned.

Incidentally, ministers are particularly sensitive about publications put out by departments. Even the most obscure of documents can contain embarrassing 'expert' comments or ambiguous facts – often stuck in an obscure annex. Commentators will then use the document to attack a minister – even though he or she may never have seen it. Of course such documents must still be published, but ministers are entitled to be warned about possible problems and given an opportunity to prepare their comments. All documents should therefore be read in detail by someone other than their author to check for problems.

And we must be particularly careful when supporting our minister in 'the box' in the House of Commons, or sitting in a committee room anywhere in Parliament. In particular, it is a dead giveaway if we put our head in our hands when our minister is asked the one question that we have particularly dreaded.

SUBMISSIONS

Your formal advice to ministers, or requests for approvals and authorisations, will be contained in a written submission. Emails, PowerPoint presentations and conversations are excellent ways of taking discussions forward but they should never be used for important decisions.

Each department has its own preferred submission structure, but a very good one, used by a number of departments, meets most ministers' preferences by telling them very quickly why they are reading your advice, and what you recommend. If your advice immediately sounds sensible, and the issue is not too contentious, they then need to do no more than glance at – or they can even ignore – the reasons for your recommendation. But, if they need to, they can dive into the subsequent detail. This leads to the following structure:

- Issue;

- Recommendation;

- Timing;

- Background;

- Argument;

- Presentation.

If the issue is a simple one, you can condense the issue, recommendation and timing into one paragraph, but the other items should always be kept separate, even if each is quite short. But be aware that some ministers prefer always to read the supporting detail, and their wishes should be respected, even if the result is that they ask that their submissions are lengthier than you feel sensible, or structured in a different way. It is vital that ministers should be given the facts and arguments that they believe necessary so that they can take good decisions in which they have real confidence.

Before starting to draft, consider carefully whether you are seeking to formulate policy or helping promote, defend or implement it. The tone, substance and length of your submission will be greatly affected by this decision. It can then be helpful to prepare a first draft of the submission in the following order (rather than the one suggested above for the final draft):

- Presentation: First, you should draft any press notice that might be needed to communicate the decision that you are recommending. It may be too soon to show your draft to a minister but, if the draft comes easily then the rest of the submission will probably flow quite naturally. On the other hand, policies that are hard to understand, and hard to defend, are often flawed. Deal also with other presentational issues, such as the method of any announcement, media handling, and so on.

- The Issue: A brief statement of the problem or the decision that needs to be taken.

- Background: Provide sufficient facts and a summary of the story so far, including a rehearsal of previous ministerial decisions and correspondence. If referring to documents, summarise or attach them. But consider how much the minister already knows or will remember, for it is often possible to reduce the background to a couple of sentences.

• Argument: The considerations, based on the (above) background, which lead you to clearly identified conclusions and recommendations. Summarise all the reasonably possible options and deal (perhaps briefly) with the merits and demerits of each one.

• Recommendations: Now summarise your conclusions and recommendations, cross-referenced to the appropriate paragraphs of the argument section. If possible, you should phrase your advice so that the minister can just say 'yes' or 'no'. Do not merely recommend a discussion with officials. It is important that you should recommend a specific course of action or decision, taking into account ministers' declared policies and political agenda. If ministers accept your recommendation then you have saved yourself and them a meeting. If not, any discussion will be assisted by the minister having a firm recommendation to discuss and test.

• Timing: A note of the timescale within which the decision needs to be taken, with an explanation if there is a need for urgency.

The final draft can then, if necessary, be re-ordered to bring the Recommendations and Timing sections up front. It can also be shortened! Because ministers are under constant pressure, you should be as succinct as possible – no more than two or three pages of typescript. If you really cannot bear to cut stuff out, then at least consider putting it in an annex. It may never get read but it might make you feel better.

 Here are some things that ministers have said about submissions.

> Officials need to be able to capture the key elements of the submission – the core message – in three or four lines at the beginning. This enables a busy minister to focus straight away on the essence of the problem and then read around it as much as he or she wishes. In most cases, submissions were too long and did not relegate subordinate issues to a few well-selected appendices. Nor did they deal with communication issues, which could often be key.
>
> —PETER HAIN

> There was a kind of risk-averse approach to briefing which saw it as dangerous to leave information out, when the key skill was to know what information to leave in.
>
> —NORMAN WARNER

> The key skill I relied on was the ability of my advisers to summarise documents accurately. These précis needed to cover not just substance but be alert to politically sensitive issues.
>
> —KENNETH BAKER

Incidentally, try not to take yourself or your advice too seriously. You may well analyse a problem in great depth and craft an elegant submission which convinces you and everyone around you of the merits of your recommendation. But issues are seldom really black and white, and the world will not come to an end if the minister disagrees with you. And even if your advice is not accepted, its preparation will certainly not have been a waste of time, for it will have prepared the minister for attacks from any commentators and political opponents who independently come up with the same conclusion as you.

BRIEFING MINISTERS AND SENIOR OFFICIALS

If a minister (or a senior official) is about to hold a meeting, take part in a discussion, or make an official visit, you will submit written briefing. It is easy to forget that the primary purpose of a written briefing is to help the reader achieve his or her objectives for the meeting. In order for this to happen, all briefings should include the following elements, preferably in this order.

- Reason for the Meeting: Provide a brief explanation of why the meeting, visit etc. was arranged and who asked for it, e.g. 'You asked us to arrange this meeting to try to resolve the disagreement between...' or 'This is another in the series of meetings in which you are meeting children's charities.'

- Directions, Agenda etc.: These are very important! The person being briefed (or their private secretary) has to know when the meeting is taking place, how to get to it and what is to be discussed. The agenda should be agreed in advance with other participants and should, in the case of a long meeting, suggest starting times for each item.

- Objectives: This is the most important part of the brief. You must clearly identify what needs to be achieved if the meeting or visit is to be judged a success, e.g. 'The objective is to get the organisation to agree that...' or 'The objective is to agree a price of £10 million or less, for [the project] completed by the end of October', or 'Your objective is to learn about the company and the industry. But the company should also be given an opportunity to lobby about its current planning difficulties (see letter of ... at Annex ...)'.

   Above all, as ever, think very carefully about whether the meeting is intended to help the minister decide his or her policy direction – in which case he or she can be encouraged to enter into a fairly open discussion – or whether the meeting is intended to help the minister achieve his or her pre-determined objectives, in which case their style will need to be more proactive or defensive, as the case may be. Meetings with other ministers should generally fall into the first category. It is a great mistake to encourage ministers to take fixed positions when discussing genuinely difficult issues with colleagues – if only because the other ministers will respond by adopting fixed positions themselves, so everybody wastes time.

- Line to Take: This is the section that the minister will have in
  front of him at a formal meeting. Consider repeating it on a card,
  printed in large type in 1.5 spacing. Provide key points that need
  to be made and then, if necessary, add defensive material such as
  areas of vulnerability and the counter arguments. The whole thing
  should be in a form that can be read out – so it should sound like
  a human being speaking to another human being. Do not include
  confidential material here, in case it too is read out!

- Participants: You should provide the forenames and surnames,
  and positions, of the principal people who will be at the meeting
  or the principal hosts of a visit. And unless the person being
  briefed knows them quite well, add a brief CV and a note of other
  important or relevant facts.

- Background: This is often the least important part of the briefing.
  In general, the length of the background should be in proportion
  to the length, complexity and importance of the meeting, and in
  inverse proportion to the knowledge of the person being briefed.
  A first, day-long visit to a major institution will therefore justify
  comprehensive background briefing, including a copy of their latest
  annual report. You may also consider using a commercial database
  or the internet. And briefing for a difficult or complex negotiation
  must include a summary of previous discussions (whether at official
  or ministerial level) as well as copies of all documents, legislation
  etc. that might be referred to. On the other hand, a second or third,
  essentially courtesy, call might require little more background
  briefing than a reference to recent news, or recently raised issues.

Finally: try to ensure that one official takes responsibility for gathering together, and clearly presenting, all the briefing for a meeting, even if several officials provide contributions. It may seem to officials that the meeting will deal with a number of different subjects, but the minister will see only one meeting and needs to be presented with one set of objectives, one agenda and one set of papers, clearly presented and flagged.

MINISTERIAL CORRESPONDENCE

You will draft replies to a huge number of letters during your career, for both your own signature and that of others. The key thing to remember is that you should draft a letter that:

- Provides a full and intelligent reply to the incoming correspondence;

- Positively, persuasively, clearly and accurately states the minister's views; and

- Clearly sets out any follow-up action.

Letters should also:

- Show that the minister appreciates what is troubling the correspondent;

- Be polite and helpful;

- Use clear, uncomplicated language and short sentences; and

- Be to the point, avoiding jargon and references to legislation
  unless they are absolutely necessary.

Minister Peter Hain told his staff that a letter to the public 'had to be in a language and style that someone, say, in a valley in Wales, rather than a corridor in Whitehall, could understand. It needed to be accurate but not technical, persuasive not assertive, sympathetic not dismissive.'

As always, you must be clear, before you start on the reply, what mode you are in. Is the correspondence part of the process through which policy is decided, or are you in 'promote/ defend' or 'implement' mode? Correspondence about policy development or policy implementation can be more interesting, because you can (or the minister can) admit uncertainty and enter into genuine debate. Defensive letters are more boring, because you want to close the correspondence. It is therefore tempting – and sometimes necessary – to draft something very short, simply saying that the correspondent's views have been noted, or rehearsing the government's position without responding to the particular points in the incoming letter. But try to do better than this. The person at the other end will almost certainly have invested a lot of time and emotion in the letter to the minister and it is awful if they just get a brush-off by way of reply. Equally, however, do not beat about the bush if, for instance, there is little or no prospect of the minister agreeing to something, including an invitation.

Now a word about mechanics. Private offices divide incoming correspondence into four broad categories.

First, there is inter-ministerial correspondence – formal letters or minutes sent from a minister in one department to a colleague in another. These are very important because they represent the main route through which policy problems are aired and resolved. An odd feature is the copy list, which is in the final paragraph. '*I am copying this letter to the Prime Minister, the Chancellor of the Exchequer ... and to Sir Humphrey Appleby* [i.e. to the Cabinet Secretariat].' When drafting the reply you should never say, '*I am copying this letter to recipients of yours*' – for this makes life very difficult for private office correspondence clerks, who will not have the original letter easily to hand.

Next, there are letters and emails to which the minister will reply. These include most letters from MPs, MEPs, members of the House of Lords, elected members of the devolved administrations, Privy Counsellors and key opinion formers. You will in time become quite expert at drafting replies to such letters. Replies to MPs' letters usually begin:

'*Thank you for your letter of [date] enclosing correspondence from your constituent, Mrs ..., [Managing Director of ... Co. Ltd] of [full address] about [subject].*'

The third category – relatively small in number – consists of MPs' and similar letters that are passed on to senior civil servants, usually agency chief executives, for them to reply in their own name. This happens only when the result is that the

correspondence is handled in a way most likely to meet the
needs of the MP and his or her constituent. The usual benefits
are that the MP and his or her constituent get a quicker reply;
the reply comes from the person who has direct responsibility for the subject matter of the correspondence, and direct
access to the facts; and there are paper handling and staff
cost savings. However, if an MP specifically asks for a ministerial reply, then this must be given. And officials should
never reply to MPs' or similar correspondence which raises
political issues, or issues on which the policy is not settled.

Then comes the largest category of all, the letters from the
public that are sent down for 'official reply'. These vary hugely
in style, content and importance. It is therefore a great mistake
to treat them all in the same way. Some will be so interesting
or important that the minister should be asked to reply. And
others will not need a reply at all. But the majority should
receive a reply, which might begin:

*'Thank you for your letter of [date] to the Secretary of State for ...
about [subject]. I have been asked to reply.'*

It can be quite tricky to draft polite replies to the numerous
invitations that reach ministers' offices. Some suggestions,
to get you started, are at Annex A.

Incidentally, it is useful to know that:

- Those honoured by the Queen become Sirs, OBEs etc. on the day
  of announcement. But it takes two or three weeks before a new
  Lord or Baroness is properly created. Until then they retain their
  former status.

- Letters to Sir Thomas Johnson begin '*Dear Sir Thomas*'. 'Sir Johnson' is wrong.

- Only Privy Counsellors, as well as most Lords etc., are 'Rt Hon.' (There used to be relatively few Privy Counsellors – fewer than 300 in the 1950s – including all current and former Cabinet ministers. But there are now nearly 700 after the addition of a large number of other *Great and Good*).

- It is best to refer to Baronesses as 'Baroness X' rather than 'Lady X', so as to distinguish them from women who become Ladies when their husbands become Sirs.

- The order of precedence (below Knights, Dames and CBs) is best recalled via the mnemonic COMB: CBE, OBE, MBE, BEM.

WRITING SPEECHES

I guess that most people are born able to write a good speech, just as they can learn any language. Unfortunately, the ability is usually knocked out of us as we become self-conscious and our working lives dominated by the written word. The following tips are intended to help those who wish to re-learn the ability to write an interesting speech, whether for a minister, a colleague or themselves.

To begin with, you must be absolutely clear whether the speech needs to be delivered in the first place. Speeches are very time-consuming, both in their preparation and in the travel time to and from the venue. Remember that ministerial speeches need to tread a fine line between being dull and being dangerous. Are you sure that the minister will have something interesting and/or original to say, and will not be unnecessarily political or controversial? If so, is the audience the right one? Will there be an opportunity for publicity?

If in doubt, remember how embarrassing it was when Prime Minister Tony Blair was slow hand-clapped by the Women's Institute. Commenting many years later, Polly Toynbee noted that:

> Week in, week out, flotillas of ministers stand up in front of audiences of all sorts and read out speeches badly written by someone else, platitudinous and patronising ... All organisations are thrilled to get a headline minister to speak as a crowd puller ... In the audience will be workers, professionals and experts [who] will know a hundred times more about the subject than he does. [After a very predictable and boring speech, the first or second questioner] begins to explain how life is out there ... Suddenly the meeting springs into life. The minister starts for the first time to speak like a normal human being ... there is a dialogue. The minister listens. ... when out of the shadows steps the ministerial minder, pointing to his watch. Before you know it, the great man has gone. What does he leave behind? A very angry room. ... The minister's visit has had precisely the opposite effect of that intended. Cynicism about politics is redoubled.

Even worse, all too many invitations are from organisations that need to fill an after-dinner slot or something of the sort. The last thing they want is a thoughtful speech about the weighty issue of the day – especially if the content might be critical of the community to which the audience belongs. Let's face it: half the audience will be tipsy – or worse – and the majority will certainly want to be entertained. Leave these challenges to professional after-dinner speakers. I have only once agreed to speak at an evening function, and performed so abysmally that I swore never to do so again. If a minister wants to appear for political reasons, or to raise his or her profile, then let the special adviser write the speech. He or she will know more jokes than you do.

But of course a properly prepared speech, delivered at the right time to the right audience, can be highly effective. As ever, planning and preparation are key.

First, remember your three duties and decide which you are carrying out when drafting the speech. Is the minister going to talk fairly freely about possible policy developments? Or are you helping to promote or defend ministers' policies? – in which case a more barnstorming approach will be needed. Or maybe you are even in implementation mode, which would require a quite different approach again. But do bear in mind that many audiences object to simply hearing the party line. A more considered, thoughtful and consultative speech will generally go down much better.

Second, you need to identify those one or two key messages that you and/or the speaker want to leave in the minds of the

audience. What do you want them to do differently after hearing the speech? What do you want them to remember some
days afterwards?

Third, you should find out what the audience wants to
get out of the speech. The easiest way to do this is to ask
the event organiser what will go down well, what information needs to be put over and what will please the audience.
Your one or, at the most, two key messages can then be nicely
wrapped so that the audience is first made receptive to them
– especially if the messages are likely to be unwelcome or
surprising.

Take particular care correctly to define and describe the
nature of the speech. A 'keynote address' should include the key
points that will be the main topics for discussion for the rest
of the conference. An 'opening address' will set the scene or
set out the government's position as a prelude to more detailed
speeches. In this case you should take care that the minister's
comments will not duplicate any other opening remarks by
the chair or host.

When you have decided what you want to say, then plan
your **structure**. You can do much worse than stick to the
traditional:

- Tell them what your main message will be; then

- Deliver the message; and then

- Tell them what the message was!

There may be other ways of structuring a speech, but no other way works every time, or leaves such a clear impression.

Drafting: Actually, the worst thing you can do is either 'draft' or 'write' a speech. If a speech reads well, especially to colleagues, it will sound stilted and boring. You should simply put your speech structure on the table in front of you, and start typing as fast as you can. If you get stuck, think about the audience and talk about them and the issues that face them. Use plenty of anecdotes and illustrations, avoid long lists, and ditch detailed statistics in favour of easily grasped facts (e.g. 'last year we doubled our exports to X' rather than 'in 2015 our exports to X were 92 per cent up on 2015'). Above all, get some emotion into it, and some power. The result will be much more interesting – and more natural.

Then check the typed text for unclear or misleading phrases; remove platitudes and generalities; and check that it consists only of sentences that are less than two lines long. Finally, read the whole thing through out loud, to make sure that it trips off the tongue fairly easily. Do not, as has happened, ask a minister to describe how he has 'instituted an epidemiological survey'.

You will of course need to show the draft to colleagues affected by its content. But, unless it contains a major statement of government policy, try to avoid showing it to senior colleagues. They will only start fretting about the colloquial language and the split infinitives, and turn the whole thing into an essay that will read well but sound awful.

On the day, always check the technology. Is the speaker

familiar with the microphone and/or teleprompter, and does it work? Ditto the projector and/or video player. Does he or she know how to control them?

It is also worth listening carefully to the speech, even if you know every word off by heart. Try to tune into the minister's speech patterns, sense of timing etc. You will never mimic them exactly, but it will help you when you next settle down to dictate a speech.

And afterwards check how the speech was received. If it went down badly, you can blame the speaker. Either way, you will learn something for the future. But don't fret if the speech really bombed. It happens to us all.

LOBBIES AND LOBBYISTS

You will meet a lot of people who are trying to get the government to act in a way that will work to their advantage. A small number will lobby on behalf of others – and especially on behalf of those who cannot lobby for themselves. And occasionally – but probably not very often – you will come across a professional lobbyist working on behalf of a client.

The key thing to remember is that, in one respect, they all want the same thing – which is for their message to be understood. They will therefore react very badly, and pester you much more, if they think that you are being over-defensive, or cannot be bothered with them, or that they are being fobbed off. So always put yourself in their shoes, emphasise that you do understand their concern, and that their views will genuinely be taken into account.

Campaign letters – hundreds or thousands of them – can be a logistical nightmare. You first need to decide whether they need a response. It is better, of course, if you can reply to each one, especially in view of the principle outlined above. But individual responses are usually out of the question. Maybe you can send a really well-written response to the organisation that has organised the campaign, and they can distribute it in their newsletter? Or even better, these days, you might use blogs, tweets etc.

Serious lobbyists will ask for a meeting and you should generally agree to such requests, partly to show that you have not closed your mind, and partly because a good discussion can often lead to surprising insights that might help you crack the underlying problem. And don't get upset if they ask to see 'someone senior' or a minister. After all, they want to know that their message is getting beyond you, and how better than to deliver it in person? If the person lobbying is sufficiently senior, or the campaign is high profile, then you should ensure that they are seen at an appropriately high level. The exact level is always a question of fine judgement, but the aim, as always, should be to reassure the caller that the department and its minister are taking them seriously. If that needs a minister, then so be it. Equally, however, I have often pointed out to lobbyists that they will only get a few minutes of a minister's time, or of the time of a senior official, whereas they could spend much longer, and have a more fruitful dialogue, with the departmental expert.

Status can be a problem the other way round. Some large companies have middle or senior managers who lobby hard in support of their particular responsibility. A research director, for instance, might press you to spend huge sums supporting research and development in their area, whilst a property manager might want you to relax planning laws. It is always worth checking that they have the full support of their own senior colleagues. For instance, does their chairman, who so often rails against excessive government expenditure, really support the proposed £100 million government research programme? Or does he really want rid of green-belt controls, bearing in mind his vehement opposition to the expansion of a computer laboratory in his pleasant Cambridgeshire village? If so, let him come in and tell ministers to their faces. Such meetings add small pleasures to otherwise dull days.

You need to be tougher with those who ask for repeat meetings when they have very little new to say. Consider carefully whether you have yourself done what you should to keep them in touch with developments. If so, then you may simply have to refuse a meeting that is going to be a waste of everyone's time – but maybe soften your refusal with an offer to meet again at a more sensible time.

And watch out that a meeting does not backfire on the lobbyist, particularly when the minister is acting in a quasi-judicial capacity. For instance, a minister who agrees to see a party to a planning application may either then have to see all the other parties or decide against the said party in order to avoid being judicially reviewed. Much the same applies to competition and merger cases. It can be amazing how quickly the meeting idea is dropped, once the implications are explained.

Professional lobbyists (and their in-house equivalents, public affairs directors) are generally a good thing, particularly because they ensure that all the arguments are marshalled together and clearly presented. They also provide a helpful service to industrialists and others who are often surprisingly terrified of Whitehall and all the strange beings that stalk its corridors. But they can be very pushy, so you sometimes have to be quite firm in response, especially if they want repeat meetings when there is little more to be said. Luckily they are pretty thick-skinned – and why would you care if they never trouble you again? But take care to ensure that you are not refusing a meeting that might indeed have taken the debate in a useful direction. And make sure you see their client, and not just the lobbyist.

But do not let anyone outside government, however important they are, get the impression that policy is being framed with only their interests in mind. Colleagues elsewhere in government are understandably on the look-out for signs of 'departmentalitis' and all too willing to believe that you have 'gone native' and become the unwitting (and unprofessional) advocate for a particular interest. This accusation can all too easily be thrown at officials in outward-facing departments who are understandably concerned to ensure that the farmers' voices, say, or small firms' concerns, are properly understood throughout Whitehall. Take care, therefore, that you frame your arguments with other departments in such a way as to make it clear that you are genuinely seeking a decision which is consistent with wider government policy, and not narrowly focused on the needs of one client group.

It follows that you should take particular care to ensure that no one is allowed to bully either you or a minister, for instance by threatening an unwarranted appeal or judicial review. Equally, you must if necessary be prepared to take an important point of principle to the Supreme Court. Conversely, you need to be conscious of the value of the good name of the British government. The government sets out to deal fairly and straightforwardly with everyone. In particular, civil servants never bluff. If we say that we will take certain action in certain circumstances, including going to court, then we must mean it. Failure to do so damages the government's credibility.

Finally, you should never rely on oral representations when important principles, or large amounts of money, or careers, or reputations, are at stake. Telephone communication is particularly unreliable, for you lose the visual clues that add texture to face-to-face communication. So get everything written down, either in the form of a contract or as your record, copied to the other party, of what they said. For instance, if someone comes in for a meeting (with you or a minister) as a result of which the minister might make a controversial decision, ensure that there is an accurate record of what is said, and send it to the person before the decision is made. He or she will not then be able to deny it, or claim that they were misunderstood.

MANAGING YOUR RELATIONSHIP WITH THE MEDIA

Almost everybody gets almost all their information via the media, including social media. It is therefore vital, if you are to deliver your objectives, that your media relations are first class. As noted earlier, many parts of government are engaged in what amounts to a permanent campaign, so you don't want to give the media any excuse to take an unnecessarily hostile line. There is also much truth in the saying that 'you should feed the media or else they will feed on you'. You should therefore make every effort to be proactive, open and honest with the media, who will often be grateful for a clear exposition of your objectives and activities.

But keep the following warnings in the front of your mind.

The **first** and overriding rule is that you must never, ever talk to the media without first talking to your press office – who will generally talk to journalists themselves, unless you are sufficiently senior and properly authorised, trained and prepared.

Second, remember that we are not accountable to the media – nor are ministers, though you sometimes wouldn't think so from the way in which parts of the media sometimes behave. There is no difference in principle between talking to a reporter and talking to any other member of the public. You should therefore not give information to a reporter that you would not give both to any other reporter and to any other member of the public.

Third, journalists do not trust you. They may be very polite, and they may like you, but they know that you represent ministers, and they trust ministers even less. Anyway, very few civil servants are any good at giving succinct information to those unfamiliar with the subject matter. All reporters have therefore had some experience of receiving over-optimistic predictions and over-rosy judgements (because ministers and officials have a natural desire to paint themselves and their decisions in the best possible light), and over-simple, false or misleading information (because of misunderstandings arising from rapid oral communication).

Fourth, many in the national media seem to be interested in little other than entertaining their readers, and will use you, or your ministers, for that purpose if they possibly can. Therefore, unless your story is very straightforward and/or you are very experienced, aim at essentially factual media such as local press, trade journals, the *Financial Times*, and radio and TV programmes aimed at business audiences.

It follows (see **rule one**!) that you should make sure you have access to first-class advice – particularly from your department's press office, but often also from outside experts. And if you are planning a particularly significant announcement, make sure you talk to your department's special adviser(s) and the media grid team in No. 10. This is not the place to repeat all the advice that your press office and others will give you, but some of the basics are as follows:

Don't waste effort. Don't issue boring irrelevant press notices or seek media attention for trivial stories. Do get a reputation for saying things that are worth listening to. If you need to put something on the record, use the web, or issue an information note, or maybe use a Written Ministerial Statement. Save press releases for genuinely interesting and newsworthy stories.

Keep the message simple – one main argument and a couple of supporting points. Press notices, for instance, should begin with the key points you want to get across:

- What is being planned, decided, opposed or supported?

- Why is it important?

- Where is it taking place?

- Who is doing it?

- When will it happen?

- How many people will it affect?

- How much will it cost?

If you can't distil 'the news' into a headline and one or two short supporting sentences, then don't bother with a press release. You should not use the media to communicate complex messages.

When you have worked out your message, make sure it is seen and understood by anyone who might come into contact with the media.

Make sure you have answers to all the questions that a

journalist or blogger could sensibly ask. Key facts, and answers
to all the most obvious questions, should go into any press
notice. But you need to have a background 'Q&A' covering
everything else for use by anyone who might possibly be asked
about your subject. There is nothing worse than having different
people giving different answers to the same question, and it's
almost as bad if it appears, because of lack of preparation, that
you have not thought about an important aspect of the issue.

You must never, ever have any direct contact with the media
unless (a) you are properly trained, (b) you are very experienced, (c) your press office have told you that they trust you
and (d) the subject is neither novel nor contentious. Even then,
a press officer will generally accompany you, or sit beside you
when you are on the phone. If not, you must subsequently
report what you have said.

If you are to be interviewed, here are some basic rules that
you should follow:

- Clearly identify your role. Are you speaking as yourself (i.e. an
  expert on a particular issue) and only saying what you believe to
  be true and sensible? Or are you speaking on behalf of ministers
  ('The government believes' etc.)? If the latter, consider yet again
  whether you should be doing the interview at all. You may not
  defend (as distinct from explain) government policies.
  Ministers should speak on their own behalf.

- Ensure that you can answer every conceivable question
  without prevarication.

- Prepare very carefully what you are going to say, keep it simple and do not stray beyond the area you have prepared.

- Try to 'answer and move on'. In other words, especially when being interviewed on the radio or TV, first answer the question but then add a comment or story that takes the interview in a direction which allows you to get your point across. You, not the interviewer, should be in control of what you say.

- Never knowingly lie or mislead.

- If you make a mistake, correct it as soon as possible.

- Finally, when talking to a newspaper reporter, you should generally specify that you are talking '*for background*'. He or she is not then supposed to indicate that they have been briefed by a civil servant. This is so that you can avoid upstaging your ministers, and not because you are embarrassed by what you are doing or saying. (There is no point in asking to be '*off the record*'. If you say anything interesting to a reporter, they are bound to report it – which is why you should never give to one reporter any information that you would not give to any member of the public.)

MANAGING PUBLIC MONEY

After your staff team, money is your next most important resource. But special rules apply to those who are spending public money; rules that often catch out those who are more used to spending money in the private sector.

First, you must constantly bear in mind three basic rules that are designed to prevent fraud:

- The person who authorised the expenditure (i.e. entered into the contract) can never, ever be the same as the person that authorises the payment of the subsequent bill.

- You should never pay a bill 'in advance of need', that is before the goods or services have been delivered and have been found to be satisfactory.

- If there is a limit to your financial authority (i.e. you have been told that you may only spend up to £xxx), you may not circumvent this by splitting contracts and bills into a number of smaller parts.

You may be tempted, especially towards a year end when you are anxious to spend your budget, to ignore one or more of these rules. You absolutely may never do so, on pain of dismissal, even if your intentions are honourable. (There may be occasions when it does make sense to make stage payments, for instance. But you should try to avoid these and – if you feel they are justified – you should make sure (a) that they are linked to clear, measurable and acceptable progress, and (b) that your boss has also approved the payments, in writing or emails.)

Second, you must constantly bear in mind that you (through the department's Accounting Officer), and not your ministers, are accountable to Parliament for your stewardship of public funds, including:

- Regularity, which means the requirement for all expenditure and receipts to be dealt with in accordance with the legislation authorising them, any delegated authority and the rules of government accounting;

- Propriety, which is a further requirement that expenditure and receipts should be dealt with in accordance with Parliament's intentions and the principles of parliamentary control, and in accordance with the values and behaviour appropriate to the public sector (see below);

- Value for money (VFM); and

- Compliance, both with the law and with government policies and initiatives.

You cannot simply spend money because it obviously makes sense to do so. You need to ensure that Parliament has in advance voted money to be spent in exactly the way you intend to spend it, and that you do not spend more than the money that has been voted for this financial year ending 31 March. You cannot, for instance, carry unspent money forward from one year to another.

You also need to make sure that you stay within both the cash limit and the resource limit (which includes depreciation etc.). And you need to be particularly careful that expenditure on salaries and other compensation (such as that paid on dismissal, and housing allowances etc.) is fully compliant with Treasury rules – which are generally much more restrictive than those found in the private sector. You can of course ask for the rules to be disapplied when necessary, but you need to do this in advance of making the payment – not afterwards!

Programme Spend: Sop or Lever?

But there is much more to spending money sensibly than merely obeying the above rules. Money is of course a vital resource as you seek to achieve your objectives. But will you use it as a sop or a lever?

> Money may be used as a sop, or it may be used as a lever. When you use it as a sop ... you get some friendly notes in the press ... but it is gone. But if you use it as a lever it may be made to influence matters of far greater consequence than is measured even by the actual amount involved.
>
> —SIR WINSTON CHURCHILL

These words are even more true today than when they were first written. It is all too easy for both ministers and officials to kid themselves, and kid others, that they are doing good by spending money. This is particularly apparent at party conference time, when every announcement seems to have a price tag, and the larger the better.

The control of large-scale projects and programmes is dealt with elsewhere in this book, but I offer the following thoughts on the sensible use of 'programme spend' – those budgets that are delegated to individual civil servants and are often used to support those projects outside government which contribute to the government's objectives, such as promoting healthy living or regional economic development. (Other costs, such as salaries and accommodation, are known as running or administration costs.)

It is of course very tempting to throw the government's resources behind those seeking to 'do good'. But don't rush into a decision. The money will be wasted unless you ensure that the project is structured in such a way as to maximise the chances of it being successfully completed, and of its being good value for money. Pay particular attention to the following:

- Every project must have clear, worthwhile and testable objectives. ('Worthwhile' means that they make a difference in the real world. For example, you should not merely pay for a conference to be held. You should stipulate that it must attract a minimum number of delegates who must, after the conference, record that they have learned something or will take some action. In the case of larger projects, you must ensure that there is, for example, a measurable change in competitiveness or behaviour.) And you must make it clear that no grant (or a reduced grant) will be paid if the objectives are not achieved. You should in particular not spend a lot on programmes whose main purpose is to 'bring people together' (e.g. large and small firms, industry and academia). These objectives are laudable, but not worth tens of thousands of pounds, let alone millions. Far better, buy them all a nice lunch!

• Every project must be 100 per cent 'owned' outside government. We may feel very committed to the work, but our role is to be a supporter and banker, not the entrepreneur or owner. The more we get involved, the more we risk reducing the sense of ownership, and hence the commitment, of the true project managers. In particular, every project must have a clear champion – one person outside government who is personally committed to seeing it through to a successful conclusion. And there should be clear evidence that larger projects are backed by a senior figure who is unambiguously committed to exploiting the results of the project. We cannot afford to bankroll the ambitions or hunches of staff who are not fully backed by their directors.

• Remember in particular that you cannot give money to a body of which you are a member. If your job requires you to join a board that is supervising a programme or project, you must make it crystal clear that you are only doing so as an observer. Remember too the related point that you must not behave in such a way as to suggest that the government might stand behind a body which is receiving public funds. If you were to do this, you might be deemed to have become a 'shadow director', in which case you might find that the taxpayer has become liable for the whole of the debts of the body concerned.

- Similarly, there should be clear evidence of financial commitment from outside government. Be particularly wary if you are asked to pay more than 25 per cent of the cost of a project. This suggests that no one else is willing to put much of their money where their mouth is. This is especially true of collaborative projects where the non-government proportion is shared between several participants, none of whom, it often turns out, are much bothered about whether the project succeeds.

- You should be particularly reluctant to accept that government money might be necessary to 'pump prime' a project that will eventually stand on its own feet. You need to ask why someone should support the project once the pump has been primed, when they are not prepared to do so now.

- Take care if you are asked to support interesting experimental work in, say, one school or one company or one local authority area. If the experiment appears successful, are ministers committed, and will the financial and managerial resources be available, to implement the change nationwide?

You must set up robust monitoring arrangements (which will survive your moving on to another job) if money might need to be repaid to the government after the final grant has been paid over. Examples include loan agreements and grants to create employment, which are repayable if the jobs disappear within a certain number of years.

PARLIAMENTARY BUSINESS

Ministers, assisted by their civil servants, are primarily accountable to Parliament, not to the media or anyone else. Ministers'
accountability takes two forms. First, Parliament can question
and debate both policies and behaviour. Second, it exercises
close control over government expenditure.

Separately, those civil servants who have been appointed
as Accounting Officers are directly accountable to Parliament
for the expenditure of their department or agency. And many
senior officials appear with or on behalf of their ministers
when being questioned by Select Committees.

The Parliamentary Timetable

A new parliament begins after every general election.

A new parliamentary session begins with the Queen's
Speech in May each year, and, in the absence of an election,
runs through to the following April, with a big gap for the
summer recess. Bills cannot normally be carried over from one
session to another but there are a growing number of exceptions to this rule, about which you can get advice from your
parliamentary branch.

The parliamentary day usually begins, with prayers, at 2.30
on Mondays, 11.30 on Tuesdays and Wednesdays, and 9.30 on
Thursdays and Fridays. Officials are not allowed into 'the box'
near their ministers until five minutes later, when (except on
Fridays) First in Order Oral Questions begin (usually abbreviated

to First Order PQs or Oral PQs). These normally last one hour, but only thirty minutes on a Wednesday – when they are followed by thirty minutes of Questions to the Prime Minister.

Next come Urgent Questions. These are nowadays allowed quite often – on average around once a week – and typically last around forty minutes. These are then followed by Statements. There may be none but there is usually one, and often more than one, and each can last for up to forty-five minutes or an hour, much to the frustration of ministers and their officials waiting for subsequent business. The first Statement on a Thursday is usually the Business Statement by the Leader of the House, who needs briefing on Early Day Motions – see further below.

Next (briefly) come applications to the Speaker for Standing Order 20 (i.e. Emergency) Debates. Applications are rarely accepted but if they are, they take place later that day or the next day. And then there might be a Ten Minute Rule Bill – an opportunity for an MP to speak for ten minutes on a topic that they regard as important. Another Member (but not a minister) might reply, again for up to ten minutes.

And then at last we get to debates on Bills, opposition motions and so on, which run through to a final thirty-minute Adjournment Debate.

In parallel with the main Chamber, there are frequent Westminster Hall debates on non-contentious business. These sittings actually take place in the Grand Committee Room just off Westminster Hall and are usually held on Tuesdays (a.m. and p.m.), Wednesdays (a.m. and p.m.) and Thursdays (p.m. only).

There can be considerable variations on the above – especially as Parliament from time to time experiments with different formats and timetables. Your parliamentary clerk will keep you right, and will give you the phone number of the police officer at the back of the Speaker's chair, where ministers enter the Chamber and officials enter the box. He or she is unfailingly helpful and will in particular be able to tell you the time before which your business is unlikely to start, so allowing you to maximise your time in a nearby coffee bar or, if in the middle of a panic, in your office.

Parliamentary Questions

It cannot be stressed too strongly that ministers and officials are under a duty to be both open and absolutely honest when answering questions from parliamentarians, whether at question time, in debate or in correspondence. Put simply, MPs are entitled to straight answers to straight questions.

Written Questions are those where both the question and the answer are written, and they are part of the process by which MPs gather information from the government. They tend not to be used for political point scoring because they do not usually receive much media attention. Therefore, unless the question is obviously antagonistic, ministers will usually reject draft answers that are deliberately cagey. In general, it is best to aim for accuracy and brevity in both the draft reply and the background note. And if the reply is likely to fill more than two columns of Hansard, you might suggest that the answer is that 'I will write to the Hon. Member and will place a copy of my letter in the Library'.

On the other hand, Parliament is a political arena and indeed some parliamentary 'questions' – and especially Oral Questions – in substance amount to little more than political point scoring. Therefore, as noted above, it is perfectly proper for a civil servant to prepare a draft letter, Statement or Parliamentary Answer that praises the government's policies, and it is perfectly proper for our drafts to omit facts and arguments that might cast doubt on the appropriateness of those policies. But even in these circumstances, any factual element to the answer has to be accurate and the answer, when read as a whole, must not mislead the reader.

The more pedantic of my colleagues will wish me to point out that many Oral Questions are actually written, in the sense that they appear on the Order Paper and are not repeated before the minister rises to reply to them on the floor of the House. But the answers are oral, as are Supplementary Questions and their answers. There are therefore two stages to preparing answers to these Oral Questions. First, there is the easy bit, drafting a short answer to the Question as tabled. Second, and much harder, you have to anticipate what lies behind the Question by suggesting key points to make and answers to give to possible Supplementaries.

There are also Topical Oral Questions, where the MP can ask about any topical issue that is within the department's responsibilities. There needs to be prior liaison between the minister's offices, the Parliamentary Private Secretaries, the press office and officials in order to identify topics which may come up, and briefing then needs to be provided.

Prime Minister's Questions are rather similar to Topical Questions in that they are almost always open questions about the PM's engagements, so allowing the questioner to ask Supplementaries about any issue that is causing controversy. You should therefore offer briefing (via parliamentary branch) if your subject has become newsworthy, providing only one or two key points to make, so that the Prime Minister can forcefully and succinctly deal with any attack. Do not provide politicised material. This will be done by your special adviser and staff in No. 10. And you should provide only as much defensive material as is necessary to keep the Prime Minister from making a serious mistake. No. 10 do not expect perfect briefing, for time is too short, but they will complain – as I once saw – if 'the material was too lengthy, concentrating on detail inappropriate to Prime Minister's Questions, and therefore failing to make the main points effectively'.

When dealing with all Parliamentary Questions (PQs) you should remember that the Ministerial Code makes it very clear that ministers must not knowingly mislead Parliament or the public, and should be as open as possible with Parliament and the public, withholding information only when disclosure would not be in the public interest, which should be decided in accordance with any relevant statute law and current open government law and practice. Ministers also have a duty to give Parliament and the public as full information as possible about the policies, decisions and actions of the government. It is our responsibility to help ministers fulfil these obligations, and information should never be omitted from a draft reply simply because its disclosure could lead to political embarrassment or administrative inconvenience. But of course potential problems should be highlighted when the draft reply is submitted to the minister.

It is different, of course, if the requested information is classified, or has been given in personal or business confidence. Ministers should be advised to refuse to answer any question that calls for such information, on the grounds of commercial confidentiality etc. An MP will sometimes, inadvertently or deliberately, show interest in an issue, the full exposure of which would be seriously damaging to the nation or to one or more individuals or businesses. In these circumstances it is sometimes possible for a minister to meet the MP in question and explain the need for discretion – for the time being at least. If necessary, there can be consultation on 'Privy Council terms' between a Cabinet minister and a senior member of the opposition.

It can be interesting to debate whether honesty is required in certain hypothetical situations. But these circumstances are very unlikely to apply to any of us at any time in our career. In short, therefore, ministers must always be given answers that are neither dishonest nor misleading. It is not clever to do something else; it is unprofessional and wrong.

Finally, in this section, here is some advice from a former minister.

> I disliked banal 'lines to take' which seemed to be presented as standard platitudes, when the briefest thought would indicate that any

opposition could attack and undermine them. What I wanted was an imaginative way of taking an argument forward, and something to say if challenged on a key sensitive area. The responses needed to be inventive, bold and politically aware, not safe, dull and vulnerable.

—ESTELLE MORRIS

Urgent Questions

Your job is to prepare clear briefing for the Speaker so that he or she can decide whether the Question should be allowed. The briefing usually has to be prepared in a great hurry. Urgent Questions can be tabled only an hour or two before the beginning of the parliamentary day, and the Speaker needs to be briefed only minutes later, so time can get ridiculously short. It is vital that you are contactable if there is any chance of an Urgent Question being asked in your area.

It follows that the briefing should be very short and essentially factual, containing (if appropriate) enough information to demonstrate that the matter has already been well aired, or that the matter is not urgent, or that it is not the direct responsibility of the government. Indeed, if it looks as though an Urgent Question might well be allowed, ministers will often volunteer a Statement (see below) so as to avoid appearing to be forced into answering to the House.

You will know within a few minutes whether the question has been allowed. If it has, then you will need to move very quickly to prepare your minister for the session, which begins after Oral PQs and lasts around forty minutes.

Standing Order 20 (Emergency) Debates

Your role is to provide briefing so that the Speaker can decide whether to hear the application for an emergency debate, and if the application is heard, whether to accept the request. The MP's application can take up to a maximum of three minutes. If the application is successful, you will have to prepare for a full-scale debate either that evening or (you hope) the next day.

Early Day Motions

These statements of opinion signed by MPs are seldom debated, but you will need to brief the Leader of the House on them. And if the opposition front bench table an EDM contrary to government policy, you will quickly have to draft an amendment.

Ministerial Statements

Statements are normally made about major issues and developments that are likely to attract much attention both in Parliament and in the media. They are major events and take high priority.

The word 'Statement' is a little misleading in that the Statement itself (which is read out by the minister – and almost always a Cabinet minister) is always followed by a grilling by interested MPs from both sides of the House. The Statement itself therefore needs to be drafted with great care so as to ensure that it is clear, informative and concise, and contains no hostages to fortune. The minister's private office will clear the draft with No. 10 and a copy of the Statement is then usually given to the opposition fifteen to thirty minutes before it is due to be made. A Lords minister will usually repeat the Statement in the House of Lords. As well as drafting the Statement, you will need to prepare thorough briefing for the Supplementary Questions in both houses.

By the way, if your minister wants or needs to make an announcement that does not justify a Statement, you should consult your parliamentary branch about tabling a Written Ministerial Statement. Copies are made available the next day in the Vote Office, and the Statement also appears in Hansard.

Adjournment Debates

These daily debates allow MPs to draw attention to constituency and other matters. It is often the case that there are no other MPs in the Chamber, and the minister will usually wish to respond sympathetically to what is said. You will need to provide a closing speech (about ten minutes' worth), which the minister will amend or embroider once he or she has heard the opening speech, and you will need to supply background briefing.

At least one official will need to be in 'the box', and if you miss your last train then the private office will arrange to get you home. However, if the debate is likely to be in the small hours, and the minister is familiar with the subject, you might be let off!

Timed adjournment debates also take place on the last day of each parliamentary term. Eight topics are selected by ballot at least two days beforehand and the debates are otherwise broadly similar to the daily debates.

House of Lords Business

Procedures in the House of Lords are broadly similar to those in the Commons, but they vary considerably in matters of detail. For instance, I can never remember the difference between starred and unstarred questions. So don't assume anything but check with the private secretary to the minister concerned, and double-check with parliamentary branch. If the two of them agree then you have probably been given accurate information. If they disagree then get them to sort it out!

Generally, of course, the Lords are much more civilised than the Commons, and you get much more notice of most business. But do not underestimate the Lords. Many of them are real experts, and many of them are very experienced politicians. Also, government spokesmen and women in the Lords have wider portfolios than their counterparts in the Commons. These two factors together mean that your drafting and briefing has to be of very high quality.

Bills and Standing Committees

Bills (i.e. draft legislation) go through a number of stages, summarised in this chart:

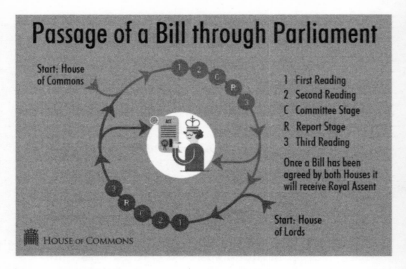

In more detail, the key stages are as follows.

- Your minister gets policy approval and drafting authority from Cabinet colleagues. This means that the parliamentary draughtsman can start work, having been instructed by your departmental solicitor, who is in turn instructed by you.

- Your minister then gains collective agreement that the Bill will form part of the legislative programme and (unless it is relatively minor and uncontroversial) it is announced in the Queen's Speech.

- There then follows Introduction and First Reading (usually a formality).

- Second Reading then triggers a major debate on the merits of the Bill.

- Committee Stage follows, in which a General Committee – usually a Public Bill Committee – examines the legislation in great detail. (Committees of the Whole House are used for the Committee Stage of certain major Bills, particularly on constitutional matters.)

- Next comes Report Stage, in which the Bill as amended in committee is reported back to the whole House, and again debated, and possibly further amended.

- Finally, for the moment at least, there comes Third Reading, following which the Bill is approved for onward transmission to the Lords (if it began in the Commons) or to the Commons (if it began in the Lords).

Then the whole process is repeated in the other House. If the Bill has not been amended in the other House then it goes on to the monarch for royal assent, whereupon it becomes an Act of Parliament and part of the UK's body of primary legislation. If it has been amended then it ping-pongs between the two Houses until they agree on a text, whereupon it then goes forward for royal assent. It is important to note that the legislation often, indeed usually, does not come into force straight away. The commencement date(s) of the various provisions in the Act may be found either in the Act itself or else in Orders which are made under the Act – see further below.

It will be clear from the above that taking a Bill through Parliament is a major and high-profile task, always entrusted to a separate Bill team. If you get anywhere near this process, you must start by reading the detailed information and instructions which your department will make available to you. You should also go to see, and listen carefully to advice from, the Cabinet Secretariat and your parliamentary clerk. And take care that you have enough resources, in the form of people and IT, photocopiers etc. The workload can be huge and urgent, especially during Committee Stage.

Secondary Legislation

You are much more likely to get involved in drafting secondary or delegated legislation – that is, Statutory Instruments (usually Orders and Regulations) that are made under the authority of previously enacted primary legislation. There are two types of Statutory Instrument, and the form that you need to use will be specified in the associated primary legislation:

- Affirmative instruments: both Houses of Parliament must expressly approve them.

- Negative instruments: become law without a debate or a vote but may be annulled by a resolution of either House of Parliament.

In both cases, Parliament's room for manoeuvre is limited. Parliament can accept or reject an SI but cannot amend it.

English-Only Legislation

The procedures described above became much more complex in 2015 with the arrival of EVEL (English Votes for English Laws) Standing Orders. Taken together, the Orders add a layer of complexity to the work around Bills and delegated legislation because of the need to provide information about territorial application and devolved competency. The procedural hoops also add a good deal to the effort needed in ensuring that ministers and officials in the Bill team are fully aware of how and when the Standing Orders bite, and of the choreography involved at each stage. No one wants to be criticised by the Speaker for failing to bob up or nod or whatever at the right time! The key thing, as ever, is to seek and take advice from your departmental experts.

Select and Grand Committees

Select Committees oversee the work of individual departments, and often call officials to give evidence. There are also some specialised Select Committees, such as the Public Accounts Committee and the European Scrutiny Committee.

The Scottish, Welsh and Northern Irish Grand Committees operate along similar lines except that, understandably, they frequently hold meetings in respective territories rather than in Westminster.

Select Committees are appointed for a whole parliament and so become experts on their subject matter. Party differences are usually (but not always) much less important than, for instance, in main Chamber business, and there is usually a good deal of consensus. Select Committees therefore deserve considerable respect.

Having decided what subjects it will look at, a committee will generally call for written evidence from outsiders, and a position paper from the department. It will then take written and oral evidence before preparing a report for the whole House. These are important documents to which ministers are expected to respond in writing.

If you are asked to prepare evidence for, or brief a colleague who is to appear before, or appear yourself before, a Select Committee then you should carefully read all the guidance that is available from your finance division and your parliamentary branch. If you or a fellow official is giving evidence then your minister will require you to follow 'the Osmotherly Rules'. These are contained in a document entitled 'Departmental Evidence and Response to Select Committees', a copy of which you should obtain. Put shortly, you may describe and explain the reasons which caused ministers to adopt existing policies but you should not give information which undermines collective responsibility or get into a discussion about alternative policies. In particular, you are not allowed to divulge:

- Advice given to ministers by officials;

- Information about interdepartmental exchanges on policy issues, the level at which decisions were taken, or the manner in which ministers consulted their colleagues;

- The private affairs of individuals, including constituents;

- Sensitive commercial or economic information; and

- Information about negotiations with other governments or bodies such as the European Commission.

The clerk to the committee will usually give you a good idea of what is needed (if you are preparing a memorandum) and will try to predict the likely line of questioning (if you are appearing in person). The key things to remember are:

- Be brief;

- Be as helpful as you possibly can;

- Be truthful and accurate, and say if you do not know the answer. (Correct any mistakes or misleading answers as soon as possible afterwards. This is often necessary, and committees understand that mistakes are made under pressure);

- Be tactful about having greater knowledge than the committee (if you do!);

- Maintain self-control, even under provocation;

- Do not tell jokes;

- You appear on behalf of your minister, who must agree your proposed response;

- Your minister is responsible for what information is given to the committee and for defending his or her decision as necessary;

- You may not publish written evidence – it belongs to the committee;

- You may publish your response to a committee report, but only after it has been received by the committee.

Petitions

There is a Petitions Committee that looks at e-petitions submitted online by members of the public. These have sharply raised the impact and hence the political importance of petitioning. The committee seeks observations from departments before deciding which e-petitions should be debated in Parliament. But it is worth noting that e-petitions do not replace the ancient paper petition process. Paper petitions can be presented with only a single signature and can be useful in drawing attention to local or small-scale concerns.

Parliamentary Control of Expenditure

Students of history will recall that the Commons' control over the Crown, and subsequently over the Executive, was exercised through control over expenditure. This control is still jealously safeguarded by MPs, including through the Public Accounts Committee, to which 'Accounting Officers' (usually Permanent Secretaries) are directly accountable for the propriety and value for money of the department's expenditure. Civil servants may therefore only spend money if they comply with statutory constraints and detailed rules which are not found in the private sector and which can sometimes seem irksome and frustrating. In particular, it is always necessary to ensure that expenditure is permitted by, and within the limits set by, both the Treasury and your finance division. It is absolutely wrong, and a serious disciplinary offence, to break or circumvent these expenditure controls.

In addition, MPs are understandably concerned to ensure that both ministers and civil servants avoid wasting or profiting from the taxes that are extracted from their constituents – many of whom are not well off and who would rightly object if civil servants either wasted their money or used it to fund an extravagant lifestyle, whether on or off duty. Put bluntly, those who want to be generously paid, or to operate a generous expense account, should not become civil servants.

The Public Accounts Committee, in particular, is quite properly intolerant of wasteful expenditure, and of decisions that cannot be supported by careful evaluation and comparison. The committee deliberates with the benefit of hindsight, and can therefore seem intolerant of risk-taking and of the need to negotiate in uncertain conditions and against tight deadlines. The correct response is not to become risk-averse, but rather to ensure that the reasons for important decisions are properly documented and supported by appropriate professional advice. With a little planning, this can be done even if the decision in question needs to be taken against a very tight deadline. Do not be surprised if a failure to take these elementary precautions is regarded with considerable suspicion by both the PAC and other observers.

WORKING WITH COLLEAGUES IN THE DEVOLVED ADMINISTRATIONS

Devolution raises many fascinating questions and problems but, in truth, most of them are mainly of interest only to academics and constitutional specialists. There is no reason why most of us should not retain sensible, co-operative and non-adversarial relations with colleagues working for the devolved administrations.

The key thing, of course, is to show respect for countries which are proud of their national structures, institutions and industries, and of the ways in which they are very different from England. Devolution is hardly a new phenomenon. The Act of Union 1707 provided that Scotland's separate legal system, church and education system should continue to be respected. And it is a mistake to worry too much if politicians in Scotland, Wales or Northern Ireland take decisions that are different from those taken by their colleagues in Westminster. Indeed, diversity is not an unintended consequence of devolution. It is the whole point of it.

The relationship with the devolved administrations should be entirely co-operative, and based on free and effective communication. If it would be helpful to share information on a confidential basis, you should not hesitate to do so, as long as the confidentiality is made clear to your colleagues. Tensions will no doubt arise – for instance where, say, the Scottish interest in an EU negotiation is not the same as the wider UK interest. But these problems will be reduced, not exacerbated, by clear and open communication.

Open and effective communication also ensures that colleagues are not surprised by Whitehall announcements, followed as they always are by questions such as 'What are you doing on this in Wales?' Colleagues can respond constructively, even if they are pursuing different policies, as long as they have prior warning.

Above all, you must not be patronising. You should ask whether a devolved administration wishes to act in a certain way, and not suggest that they should do so or, even worse, tell them to do so.

The position concerning legislation is as follows. Although the UK Parliament retains the authority to legislate on any issue, whether devolved or not, the convention is that Westminster will not normally legislate with regard to devolved matters in Scotland without the consent of the Scottish Parliament. This convention does not apply to incidental or consequential changes to Scottish law where the purpose of the new law is reserved to the UK Parliament, but there should always be close consultation with Scottish colleagues, whatever the constitutional position. The National Assembly for Wales also has a limited ability to pass primary legislation.

As always, of course, look at more detailed and formal documents, including the formal concordats with the devolved administrations, and consult experienced colleagues, if it looks as though a serious problem might be developing.

By the way, it is important to understand the respective roles of the post-devolution institutions. The Scotland Office, the Wales Office and the Northern Ireland Office are London-based departments headed by Secretaries of State who are members of the UK Cabinet. The Scottish Executive, the Welsh Assembly government and the various Northern Irish departments are the executive bodies that report to ministers accountable to the Scottish Parliament, the National Assembly for Wales and the Northern Ireland Assembly respectively.

Chapter 3

The Policy Process

GOOD POLICY MAKING:
THE POLICY PROCESS

W HAT POLICY PROCESS? The problem is that new policies, and policy decisions, can arise in, and are handled in, a multitude of different ways, as was made clear by Turner and Hulme in *Governance, Administration and Development*: 'What must be banished is any lingering idea that policy is some highly rational process in which expert technicians are firmly in control using highly tuned instruments to achieve easily predicted outcomes. Such an image is inappropriate for OECD countries let alone the developing world...'

But it is often possible to discern a number of separate key stages:

- Identifying a problem, issue or opportunity, and then researching and gaining knowledge and experience of it;

- Consultation, including impact assessment and identifying unwanted consequences;

- Analysing and exploring options; and

- Navigating Whitehall and gaining collective ministerial agreement.

You may also need to consider:

- How to handle lobby groups and lobbyists; and

- Compliance issues, and the transposition and gold-plating of European directives.

This chapter discusses each of these topics, but it is important to realise that these individual stages do not operate sequentially, but overlap as policies become firmed up. I sometimes liken policy development to a game of snakes and ladders in which occasional rapid process up the policy ladder is too often followed by rapid descent down the snake of an unintended consequence. But you will never get to your goal unless you have a clear strategy and consciously tackle each of the above key stages. You should also always refer to one or more of the checklists and sets of questions that are available to help you plan for success. A set of World-Class Policy Tests is at Annex B, and other checklists, reports and sources of advice are at www.civilservant.org.uk.

And there aren't many policy areas that don't have a European dimension. Advice on working within the EU is in the following chapter.

RESEARCH AND EXPERIENCE

To begin at the beginning, someone has to identify a problem or an issue or an opportunity. That 'someone' can include a political party (especially when in opposition and writing a manifesto), a minister, the media, a pressure group, a think tank, a trade association, an 'expert', a member of the public or a civil servant. The difficulty, therefore, is not that there are too few ideas, but that there are far too many, and it is quite impossible to run with more than a fraction of them. The natural result is that both ministers and officials are forced to spend much of their time in defensive mode, either explaining why nothing will be done or just avoiding the issue.

Some generators of ideas are more likely than others to be listened to. Ministers, obviously, are in pole position

– as long as they concentrate on a small number of initiatives and do not come up with a new idea every day. Outside experts and pressure groups can also be very effective, as long as they are truly respected by their peers. And so can civil servants, but only once they have earned the respect of their ministers.

So there are some lessons in this for the civil servant. First, try not to be over-defensive. The world is full of good ideas, hidden amongst even more bad ones. Your job is to help ministers identify the good ones, even if they are counter-intuitive, from an unusual source, or from a highly critical pressure group.

Second, take every opportunity to gain the respect of your ministers before espousing a novel idea. New ministers bestow power on those they trust. To begin with, they will prefer to deal with their political advisers and others that have previously supported them through thick and thin. They will come to trust you, as well, and bestow power on you, but only if you earn that trust over a period, and by responding positively to their agenda.

Third, seize an opportunity when it presents itself. Don't let it slip by. The best moments of your career will be when you have put an idea to a minister, or a minister has put an idea to you, and you jointly see the possibility of achieving real change. You will dash off to gather colleagues around you, and map out a dramatic and challenging strategy. You will write your ideas up that evening, rewrite them when you have calmed down in the morning, and get back to the minister, with a really positive programme, within twenty-four hours – and then you really are on your way.

There is a nice example, told by Sir Geoffrey Holland, a former Permanent Secretary in the Education Department, which illustrates much of the above. Every year – a good time ago – the British Safety Council used to send a telegram to the Prime Minister drawing attention to the accident rate in factories and saying that the situation warranted an inquiry. Every year the telegram was passed from Downing Street to the Secretary of State for Employment, then down through the department until it reached the desk of a middle manager who each year drafted the same defensive reply: 'The Prime Minister thanks the Safety Council for their telegram, the contents of which have been noted.' But one year the telegram was accidentally seen by a senior official called Charles Sisson who recognised the truth of the point that was being made, and penned a minute agreeing with the council. Out of this came the Health & Safety Executive, and our whole approach to health and safety at work was modernised.

Gaining Knowledge and Experience

It cannot be emphasised strongly enough that our advice to ministers must be based upon experience and knowledge. It should be the aim of every one of us to be the acknowledged expert in our policy area. Once we have been in the job for some time, it should be a matter of professional pride that no one else should understand our patch better than us – and that includes ministers and our line managers, even if they have the advantage of seeing a wider picture. Conversely, senior officials do not need to be familiar with all the detail that ought to be at the fingertips of others. But they should be able to hold their own in any discussion of the major issues, trends and currents that affect their policy area.

The besetting sin of civil servants is to mix too much with each other.

—SIR WILLIAM BEVERIDGE

It follows that we cannot be effective if we never get out from behind our desks. We must find a way to experience for ourselves the problems or issues with which we are dealing. Seeing, after all, is believing. We also need to be familiar with the political context of our work, and to be conscious of the world outside our own environment. Not everyone is a white-collar worker, not everyone has GCSEs and not everyone lives in the south-east of England. Indeed, 99 per cent of the world's population, and 96 per cent of economic activity, is outside the UK. We need to be aware of opportunities, trends and ideas outside our immediate experience. Without such experience we will never fully understand the arguments, emotions and undercurrents that condition the people and businesses with whom we deal. And only with such experience can we avoid the trap of recasting reality in our own image, and believing that our elegant and logical view represents the only possible view of the issue under consideration.

Gaining experience can also be great fun. For a start, it often involves travel. And although you might be criticised for travelling to interesting places at the taxpayer's expense, you will be criticised even more strongly – and with more reason – if you never get out at all. And you do not necessarily need to travel very far. I will certainly never forget my pre-dawn start sorting and delivering the Royal Mail, or the time my PA and I worked together on the production line at the Longbridge car factory. Both experiences taught me great respect for those who do such jobs, day in day out, without letting quality stand-ards slip. For instance, it would have been all too easy, with a new car coming along every eighty seconds, to let a mistake go uncorrected in order to be ready for the next vehicle, but no one did so. Such experiences also taught me the difficulty of working in non-office environments, in outdated buildings, and at times of day when none of us are at our best.

By the way, a good place to look for information is in the minds of front-line staff in departments and local authorities, and in the minds of others to whom the policy is directed. They will very often have a clear idea about why a situation is the way it is and why previous initiatives have failed. You should certainly never rely on middle or senior managers. For instance, Deutsche Bank asked 2.4 million customers and their branch managers and their junior branch staff to rate branch performance. There was a very high correlation between the junior staff's perception and that of their customers, whilst there was almost no correlation with the branch managers' perceptions and the customers'.

ANALYSIS

You should not, of course, simply accept all the 'facts' that are presented to you. Statistics can be particularly misleading.

- Aggregated statistics can look very different to the underlying figures. For instance, vehicle accident statistics generally include young and accident-prone drivers, as well as injuries to pedestrians and cyclists. Indeed, I understand that a middle-aged car driver in good weather may well be just as safe, over most long journeys in the UK, as if he or she were flying, which is a very safe form of transport.

- Different organisations will record data in different ways. The classic example is in France, where, if an elderly person is found dead without evidence of health problems, it is acceptable to attribute the death to 'old age', thus reducing the apparent incidence of heart attacks. But crime statistics can be similarly unreliable, as are many others.

- The fact that there have been no incidents does not mean that something is safe. It is possible that fewer children are now killed on our roads not because they are inherently safer than decades ago, but rather because they are so dangerous that many children are not allowed near them.

- Death and injury rates can look very different when presented as a number (e.g. number of children killed in an incident) rather than as a proportion of the exposed population per annum.

- A report of deaths caused by, for example, air pollution might include a high proportion of those whose death was already imminent, rather than deaths from amongst an otherwise healthy population.

- Isolated statistics can give a misleading impression. For instance, the radioactivity of a beach near a nuclear plant may be higher than many others, but is it also lower than other beaches that are nowhere near such a plant?

It is easy, too, to frighten people with 'science'. Seventy-six per cent of one group of adults, presented with a number of true facts about the chemical dihydrogen monoxide, concluded that government should regulate its use. The other 24 per cent presumably knew that the chemical's other name is 'water'.

Scientific 'facts' are also often anything but 'facts' as you or I would understand the term. Indeed, you can always tell good scientists by the way in which they acknowledge uncertainties, make assumptions explicit, distinguish between what is true and what is speculative, and present options.

By the way, do not be tempted, when faced with a hostile press or a one-sided lobby, to assemble your own dodgy statistics – or dodgy science – to fight them off. The inevitable result would be that those with whom you are trying to communicate would then see you as prejudiced and/or adversarial, and you might also then fail to pay insufficient attention to perfectly reasonable arguments from 'the other side'.

Moving beyond science and statistics, you must remember that it is unfortunately in the nature of our society that most correspondents, and most of the people that we meet, will present a one-sided view of an issue, drawing attention to all the relevant facts and arguments which support their case but failing, either deliberately or through sheer conviction, to take account of inconvenient facts or opposing arguments. But as you gain experience, you will quickly learn to detect the pure advocate or bullshitter.

Take care, therefore, not to be too trusting, and bear in mind the famous warning that 'he would say that, wouldn't he!' No one who is applying for a grant will tell you that they will in fact go ahead even if they do not get it, and no businessperson will tell you that the principal purpose of their latest acquisition is to build market power. Similarly, most people are reluctant to admit their errors, and their reluctance will be in proportion to the seriousness of their error. Therefore, especially if you are questioning someone's honesty, you should never merely accept their personal assurances, however convincing they may sound. Find out the facts and let them speak for themselves.

The same applies, but less strongly, to professional advisers. Lawyers, accountants and merchant bankers are employed by their clients to persuade you to do certain things. They will usually tell you the truth, but not necessarily the whole truth. They will also sometimes imply, and indeed believe, that their opinion (e.g. about the viability or prospects of a company) is a fact. If your instinct is to the contrary, then rely upon your instinct, at least to the extent of probing further.

CONSULTATION, EXPLORING OPTIONS, IMPACT ASSESSMENT AND UNINTENDED CONSEQUENCES

'The first duty of a commander is reconnaissance.' This military doctrine applies equally to hotly contested policy initiatives. The best laid schemes will certainly go badly awry unless supported by strong and open-minded consultation processes. There is excellent official guidance which you should certainly read as soon as you start thinking about tackling a policy issue. The key points are as follows:

- First, consider – and that means *seriously* consider – all the options, from doing nothing through to legislation, with improving information, codes of practice, self-regulation and economic incentives along the way.

- Second, consult – and that means consult before making firm recommendations to ministers, as well as, for instance, on any draft legislation.

- Third, if you do need to legislate, keep the regulations as simple as you can. Identify the precise problem, use plain English, provide flexibility and keep it short!

- Fourth, consider compliance (see further below).

- Fifth, provide good, clear, simple guidance to accompany the regulations.

- Sixth, if regulation appears necessary, prepare an impact assessment at each stage.

Exploring Options

So you have identified a problem or opportunity, gained relevant experience and identified all the necessary facts and opinions. What policy options are at your disposal? Put shortly, the government can do one or more of four things if it wishes to change behaviour:

- It can exhort – and '*nudge*';

- It can tax;

- It can spend – which also implies taxing or borrowing; or

- It can legislate and regulate.

Exhortation means deploying all possible presentation skills, including getting key stakeholders on side, working with the media, producing leaflets, advertising, speeches and so on. As noted earlier, presentational issues should be considered early in any policy development process and effective presentation can sometimes achieve significant policy objectives on its own. All too often, however, you need to move on and add one of the next three options if you really want to have an impact...

... But then you will find that ministers have a strong aversion to raising taxes or spending money (which are two sides of the same coin), so they prefer you to offer new legislation or regulations – until they realise that this route too can lead to huge resentment amongst those who are to be regulated, and can also have a large impact on the economy. There is much to be said, therefore, for genuinely open consultation, seeking views on the true scale of the problem and on a wide variety of ways in which it might be tackled. You must, in particular, give a good deal of thought to the way in which a new service is to be delivered, or a new regulation communicated and enforced. Central government may need to set the aims, but localism, delegation and contracting out can often lead to the delivery of more responsive, innovative and efficient services, including much-improved co-operation between local agencies. But don't forget to consult on the 'do nothing' option. It is often the best one!

Effective Consultation

There used to be a time, apparently, when the government could simply tell the public what decisions it had taken. It then became necessary to explain why the decision had been taken, which in turn led ministers to consult in advance of decision-making. Best practice is now to go even further and involve the public and key stakeholders at all stages of the policy process.

There are lots of different ways to do this and you should not simply duplicate what someone else has done before you. In particular, don't limit yourself to written communications. Discussion groups, large formal meetings, informal meetings with individuals, and the internet all have a part to play. And even when preparing formal written consultation, there are a number of choices. Have a look at the detailed advice that is available on consultation procedures, and also look at a range of previous consultation documents and choose a format that best suits your needs. Above all, remember that you are in policy-formulation or policy-implementation mode, so there is no need to be defensive. Indeed, you should positively encourage respondents to point out your mistakes and possible pitfalls. Good decision-making depends on allowing or even encouraging dissent up to the point when ministers have taken their decision. If your process is effective, and you take the responses seriously, you will find that you then avoid a very large number of traps that you would not have spotted by yourself.

You should therefore encourage those who seem to be able to take a wider view. Cultivate those who say unexpected things or comment candidly upon their organisation. Such people shine unaccustomed light on issues and can be invaluable contributors to the policy-making process. Above all, talk to those who are unhappy with your policies. They often have a good reason, which you need to bear in mind regardless of whether you ultimately change the policy, or its detail. And don't hesitate to let your minister have a short note of what you have learned. It might just make him or her think twice.

If the subject of your consultation is particularly controversial, or if you are to meet a potentially hostile audience, or hostile media, you should remember the following basic rules:

- Actions speak louder than words. The vast majority of your audience will respond wholly or mainly to the way in which you deliver your message. 'Organisational body language' is important. Do you act, write or sound patronising, worried and harassed? Or do you act and sound calm, sympathetic and in control?

- Do not dismiss concerns, however silly you think they sound. If it appears that you do not respect basic human concerns, how can you then be trusted to come up with sensible policies?

- Instead, listen carefully and emphasise your own concern. Then commit to continuing speedy enquiries, taking proper advice and reaching an early sensible conclusion on the best way forward. Stress that the process will be participatory and open, and that you will publish any scientific or other expert advice and the assumptions upon which it is based. Remember that the public will trust you much more if you admit to uncertainty, and that the public may well be less concerned about the problem than the media.

- Explain the benefits of your proposed approach. Stress that your reaction to any problem will not be 'knee-jerk', and you will not patronise or nanny the public. If regulation might be needed, explain how this will protect the public and why other options would not work. If regulation is likely to be unnecessary, stress that you believe it right that the public should be allowed to make their own assessment of the problem, and the associated costs, risks and benefits, and react as they wish.

- A small but crucial minority in your audience will be
opinion formers who will want to understand the underlying
issues and will analyse your response very carefully. Get the
majority of them to accept your credibility, and respect
your openness, and they will sustain you against much
unfair comment.

- Do not say that a particular option would be 'too expensive'.
Who are you to say that?

- Do not express concern that action to protect the public would
harm industry, for this will reinforce any concern that a risk is
being transferred from those who are benefiting from it onto
those who are not.

- Membership of advisory groups should be broadly based, and
not confined to scientists and other professionals.

- When dealing with risks to health and safety, remember that
nothing in this world is entirely 'safe'. The government's job
is to ensure that everything is 'safe enough'.

Finally, remember that there is a crucial difference between
releasing information and informing the public. The whole-
sale release of vast amounts of data does not of itself inform
anyone. There should of course be no question of hiding or
distorting information, but care should be taken to ensure that
the overall effect of the release of information is to improve

recipients' understanding of the issues (and the uncertainties) rather than simply to add to the confusion.

Impact Assessment

The first impact assessment should include a clear statement of the policy objectives as well as an initial assessment of the risks, costs and benefits of regulation, as well as why non-regulatory options – including doing nothing – are unattractive. Later assessments will build on these foundations, adding more detail and more certainty, and they will be published as part of the formal consultation process and alongside draft legislation. It cannot be stressed too strongly that IAs are very important documents, whose preparation needs to be properly planned and resourced, and started early enough to form a genuine part of the decision-making process.

Much the same advice applies if you are negotiating in Brussels. Again, there is much excellent guidance, and either you or the Commission should prepare an impact assessment – also often known as a fiche d'impact.

Unintended Consequences

It is also important, whether you are imposing taxes, spending money, drafting domestic legislation or transposing European legislation, that you take care to avoid unintended and unwanted consequences, and (if regulations are necessary) to regulate in such a way as to encourage compliance and deter evasion. Let's look first at unwanted consequences.

The key point to remember is that it is, by definition, very difficult to identify unintended consequences – and this is one of the main reasons why genuinely open-minded consultation is so important. It might help if I list the sorts of unwanted consequences that can occur:

- A risk-free food chain might raise costs (to the detriment of the poor), restrict imports (to the detriment of developing countries) or sacrifice taste and texture for the monotonous security of the can.

- Attempts to reduce sports injuries might well generate poor health as a result of reduced physical activity.

- Expensive railway safety might increase fares and charges and so divert traffic to more dangerous urban roads.

- Attempts to create risk-free childcare might reduce the availability of such care.

- The risk to a child living with inadequate parents needs to be balanced against the risk of the damage that would arise from enforced separation.

- UK-only regulation might, if it were to increase the price of UK goods, lead to cheap unregulated goods coming in from abroad.

And, anyway, people will usually adjust to whatever changes are made. Do remember that you are dealing with a dynamic situation, not a static laboratory experiment. For instance, because we each seek to arrive at our own personal balance between cost and benefit, we will intuitively adjust our behaviour to avoid, or mitigate the effect of, an increased risk, and vice versa for a reduced risk. The observed effect of an increased or reduced risk is therefore often unpredictable. This particularly applies where (as in the case of road safety) most of us have intuitively established the level of risk with which we feel comfortable. To take a simple example, if a winding road is to be straightened or widened, you would not assume that drivers (or the NHS) would pocket the value of all the increased safety. Instead, most drivers would speed up – accepting some of the risk for themselves, and transferring some of the risk to pedestrians etc.

Another aspect of the same phenomenon is that the public or business community will usually adjust their behaviour to cope with an unwelcome development, or simply just get used to it. This is why environmental groups, for instance, are so keen to stop certain developments before they become established as precedents. Their response may seem to be out of proportion to the harm done by the proposed development but it might make a great deal of sense in the wider scheme of things. Do not therefore underestimate or patronise such lobby groups.

Indeed, once a policy decision has been implemented, it can be very difficult to tell whether it was correct, and it also becomes very difficult to get back to where you began. Who knows, for instance, whether it was right to give planning permission to certain large developments? But any attempt to knock them down would cause an uproar from those who live in, work in or supply them, or from those who have simply grown fond of them (Battersea Power Station, for instance). I sometimes wonder what would have happened if our predecessors had known for certain that motor vehicles would end up causing one million deaths a year around the world. So don't get too upset when a minister takes an apparently illogical decision. The Great British public will probably find a way of adjusting to the decision, if not actually circumventing it.

Compliance

It is vital that compliance and enforcement issues are considered before any decisions are made about the scope and nature of any regulations. The legislation can be well meant, but it will quickly fall into disrepute if it has to be policed in an obtrusive way, or if the cost of its enforcement is out of proportion to its benefit. Regulations should always be transparent, targeted, consistent and in proportion to the risk, and the regulator must be publicly accountable.

Compliance is often best assured by providing incentives to encourage those causing the risk to change their behaviour. Where possible, therefore, the cost or impact of the regulation should fall upon the person causing the risk, not the person suffering it. If that is not possible then any numerical targets (e.g. for local enforcement bodies) should be concerned with reductions in the occurrence in the risk (e.g. fewer outbreaks of food poisoning) rather than increases in enforcement action (e.g. numbers of prosecutions). And don't make it obligatory for small firms to keep papers for forty years – and, yes, such a regulation did recently exist.

Watch out, by the way, for the implications for middle-class journalists. For instance, when designing policies affecting employees, think carefully about their impact on au pairs. Or when changing education policy, how will it affect Montessori schools? You attack the freedom of the press at your peril!

Finally, make sure that your solution can be implemented by those who have not been immersed in the issue in the way that you have been. Don't design systems that are subtle, clever or difficult to understand, and don't plan staff numbers and implementation timetables on the basis that all involved will be geniuses. Also, make sure that your solution is understood by those at whom it is aimed. Research can help, of course. The Business Department, investigating ineffective product warnings, found that many young people could not define the word 'fatal'. A new warning, 'solvent abuse can kill suddenly', was substituted.

TRANSPOSITION AND GOLD-PLATING – OVERVIEW

You will also have choices when it comes to transposing European directives into UK law. The process can be fraught with difficulty. Legal advice should be obtained as soon as you begin to think about transposition, which should in turn be very early in the negotiation process. Advice on lobbying and negotiating etc. in Brussels can be found in the next chapter.

You need to reconcile a number of possible tensions. One source of tension is the desire of those who are to be regulated for regulatory certainty. Small firms in particular do not want to have to go to court to resolve ambiguities or to find out how the law applies to unusual circumstances. So even if the directive itself is not very detailed (and they often are) you end up drafting to cope with every eventuality, whereupon everyone complains about the length and complexity of your proposal. It is truly a no-win situation.

Another tension arises when you try to define the businesses, employees and activities that are within the scope of the UK regulation. EU legislators often kindly leave such decisions, within limits, to national governments, but this can be a poisoned chalice. If you spread your net too wide then you will again be accused of over-regulating and 'gold-plating' the directive. But if you exempt things that you could have caught, you are then likely to face a legal challenge from the Commission or from a body, such as a consumer group, whose members might have benefited from a wider interpretation.

There is therefore often no risk-free route to implementation and you must offer ministers a range of strategies and help them choose the right one bearing in mind all the circumstances. You should not necessarily recommend the option that is legally watertight. It can often be wise to take a small risk of legal challenge in return for coming up with a solution that makes sense within our economy and society, even if it is not the route chosen by other member states.

NAVIGATING WHITEHALL AND GAINING COLLECTIVE AGREEMENT

You may be carrying out a perfect policy process, but you still have to steer your excellent and innovative proposals through the Whitehall machine and Parliament. Scylla and Charybdis have nothing on the traps you can encounter on the way.

If you are promoting anything like an innovative solution to a policy problem then be aware that you will encounter the following obstacles:

- We work within quite distinct government departments, with quite distinct budgets, and for ministers who are usually in competition with their colleagues in other departments. This encourages an over-exaggerated loyalty to the organisation, to our staff, to our budget and to our ministers, and elementary game theory teaches us that, if no one else is co-operating, it is not in our interests to co-operate with them.

- It is a firm rule that the Treasury have to be consulted before we commit resource to anything 'novel or contentious'. And if that doesn't stop us in our tracks, a colleague will soon remind us that our Permanent Secretary is directly accountable to Parliament

for the way in which we spend public money. You will not be
encouraged to innovate in a way that could cause him or her to
have to defend you in front of the Public Accounts Committee.

- Common sense, bolstered by the doctrine of collective
  responsibility, means that it is necessary to consult, often quite
  widely, before becoming committed to any significant new policy.
  Colleagues will inevitably express various concerns and, although
  it might be possible to address each of them, the effort of doing so
  can be quite daunting.

There is no easy or simple route between these obstacles, but
some lessons seem to have general applicability.

First, you need to put real effort into building a strong part-
nership with your minister, backed by the Secretary of State.
Private secretaries and special advisers can be very helpful here.

Next, involve colleagues from other departments, including the Treasury, at the earliest possible opportunity, and try
to build loyalty to the project, as distinct from natural loyalty to
departmental ministers. Remember that 'joining up' becomes
more difficult the more you involve ministers and senior officials, so tackle this problem early, not late. Encourage your
opposite numbers in other departments to get their bosses and
their minister on board, and get your minister to talk to theirs,
assuming the two of them get on reasonably well. Seek at all
times to ensure that the initiative is seen as cross-departmental.

Tackle the resources issue up front. Many ministers do not
like to get involved in resource allocation, believing that civil

servants should sort this out. But the absence of resources –
whether staff or money – can be a big problem. Don't whine
to your minister, of course, but put up a lean project plan with
necessary resources clearly identified, and get it backed. You
will have to get your finance people to comment on your plans
– and if they say that they cannot be afforded then your minister will have to decide whether to fight for new money. But let
that be the minister's decision, not yours, and not your finance
branch's. Don't let ministers complain that you never deliver,
if the truth is that they will not find the money.

Plan your consultation and media strategy with particular care. It is usually a very bad idea to be secretive. It is much
better to start discussing the idea, in a non-committal, low-
key way, with key interest groups, with academia and with the
specialist press. This allows you to confront the problems very
early on, and gets buy-in from key stakeholders. And such
openness then makes it more difficult for the national press
later to run shock-horror stories.

Keep colleagues – and especially senior colleagues – well
informed. None of them like surprises, so tell them about the
initiative, and assure them that there is strong ministerial support. Also tell them whenever another key group or opinion
former comes on board. They will be glad to be associated
with success, and less likely to cause problems.

Build a strong, diverse team, and involve outside stakeholders as much as possible. Build partnerships not only within
government but also with local authorities, the private and
voluntary sectors, with other EU member states and so on.

And make sure that a good proportion of your team have strong interpersonal skills, for these are necessary if these partnerships are to be truly effective.

Keep the thing moving. It can be difficult to regain lost momentum, and there are real lost opportunities, and real costs, associated with delay, even if they do not fall on your budget.

Will you need ministers to take a Bill through Parliament? If so, plan ahead. There is quite a queue!

Above all, have a clear, written strategy and project plan, kept up to date (for it will often change) and available to all those involved. If you can publish it on the internet, so much the better.

Gaining Collective Agreement

Ministers take a great many different types of decision, and the majority of these are of interest to ministers in only one or two departments, often including the Treasury. However, ministers need to gain the collective agreement of every department if their proposal...

- is likely to attract significant parliamentary, media or other attention, e.g. from lobby groups; and/or

- is unwelcome to ministers in another department; and/or

- requires primary legislation; and/or

- needs to be trailed in a Green or White Paper.

If you are embarking on this process for the first time then you should look at the voluminous written guidance, and there is also much to be said for mimicking the style and structure of letters and papers prepared previously. Collective agreement is obtained through Cabinet committees, usually through correspondence or, in particularly difficult cases, in meetings. The impartial committee secretariats will tell you how best to proceed but, in the case of correspondence, the process usually involves your minister writing to the chair of the appropriate committee and copying the letter to all other committee members. Your minister's private secretary should extract replies, or nil returns, from all committee members and you should then contact the secretariat to confirm that the correspondence is complete. If all goes well, the secretariat will get the chair to write to confirm the collective decision to go ahead, perhaps on certain terms. Otherwise, you or your minister will have to resolve points of disagreement before writing round again with a collectively acceptable proposal.

It is vital that both correspondence and papers should (in the case of significant, novel or contentious expenditure proposals) contain the views of the Treasury and (in the case of proposals impacting significantly on the private or voluntary sectors) contain a statement agreed with the Better Regulation Executive.

If a dispute cannot be settled through interdepartmental correspondence and discussions, the secretariat will arrange for the committee to meet and consider a paper which you will prepare, consulting those colleagues in other departments who have strong views on the issue. The paper should not be too long – three to five sides (plus annexes) is quite long enough – and it should outline the proposal, the main considerations that ministers need to bear in mind, and a precise statement of the decisions sought. Any interdepartmental disagreements should be summarised in a neutral way.

If you will need primary legislation – that is, a Bill which becomes an Act of Parliament – then you need to build this into your timetable right from the start. You need drafting authority before Parliamentary Counsel can be set to work, and you then need specific collective agreement before your Bill finds its way into the programme. It is all complex but well-trodden ground, beyond the scope of these notes. But there are plenty of people who are willing to help, and there is plenty of high-quality guidance material, which you ignore at your peril.

GUIDANCE MATERIAL, AND PRESENTATION, INCLUDING MEDIA HANDLING

Explaining your new policy or initiative to the public should be straightforward if you have successfully involved stakeholder groups, who will have stopped you making everything too complex. But do prepare draft guidance material well in advance of final announcement, for you will find that the process of seeking to explain your decisions will quickly identify where you have made mistakes.

Presenting your new policy, including media handling, should also be fairly straightforward, if you have followed the advice elsewhere in this book and considered presentational issues right from the beginning of the policy development process. It also helps if you have managed to avoid the worst of the obstacles to innovation summarised above. But don't forget that your minister will certainly want a launch of some sort, which you and your press office should jointly organise.

Chapter 4

Working with the European Union

I<small>T HAS BEEN</small> difficult, in recent years, to find a policy area that could never become the subject of a discussion at the European level. This could of course change quite abruptly following the June 2016 EU referendum, which is still in the future as this book goes to the printers. But it seems best to offer the following advice on the assumption that we stay in the EU. If we leave, it may perhaps remain of some historical interest, as well as of value to those who are charged with negotiating our exit. This chapter accordingly gives basic advice on working effectively in Europe. Also, although you can survive

quite well in Brussels without understanding the history and
every last detail of the institutions, treaties and legislation, it is
best to have some basic knowledge if you want to be truly effective. I therefore include a list of key dates in the development of
the EU, together with a guide to its institutions and processes.

INTRODUCTION TO THE
EUROPEAN UNION

The EU is neither a traditional international organisation like the
UN or the OECD, nor is it a true nation state like France or
the United Kingdom. Rather, it is a new and different form
of supranational association, which needs to be understood
on its own terms and not by comparison to other, perhaps
more familiar models. This is particularly important when
looking at European legislation, which is binding and is often
agreed by some form of majority voting. This, along with the
fact that European law has supremacy over national law – in
other words, if the two conflict, then European law wins out
– makes for a very different dynamic.

Working the European Union machine is therefore quite
different to working the Whitehall machine. Some of the more
obvious differences between the UK and Europe are as follows:

- Within the UK parliamentary system, Parliament and the
  government are uniquely powerful. Within Europe, both ministers
  and officials are negotiators, applicants or supplicants.

- There is no UK equivalent of the Qualified Majority Voting (QMV) system, or of the need for unanimity.

- Where QMV applies, one country alone cannot block progress and will usually be isolated if it tries. It makes much more sense to choose constructive engagement with other negotiators, with a view, if necessary, to assembling a blocking minority and then making it stick.

- There is no UK equivalent of the Council of Ministers or the Commission. It is a great mistake to treat the Commission as though it were simply some sort of supranational civil service – it clearly also has a political role.

- Commission officials tend to be very good or rather poor, with rather fewer moderate performers than one might expect.

- The Commission is vertically organised, so there can sometimes be poor working-level co-ordination within the Commission, whether between or within directorates-general. This gives significant power to the cabinets of the various Commissioners. Incidentally, seven of the Commissioners are also Vice-Presidents of the Commission, and each VP is responsible for bringing together a group of Commissioners with related subject responsibilities.

- It is also notable that the Commissioners, their cabinets and their officials ('Services') are very open – arguably more accessible to lobbyists and industry than their equivalents in national governments. Partly because the Services are thinly staffed, they have very little information of their own. It can be very helpful if you are the person who briefs them. But watch out for competitive lobbying from the opposition, whoever they may be.

• Relations between civil servants and Members of the European Parliament are also different. Unlike within Westminster, direct contact with MEPs of all parties (and all countries) is not only allowed, it is to be encouraged.

• UKRep (our permanent representatives in Brussels and Luxembourg) are also very happy to meet and help British lobbyists who need advice on operating the Brussels machine.

• EU officials in the Council, Commission and Parliament are almost always very pro-European, as are many of your opposite numbers in other national delegations. Even if you hate the very idea of European integration or the single currency, you may find you get a more receptive audience for your lobbying if you hide your views and couch your comments and arguments in 'communautaire' (EU-friendly) language.

LOBBYING AND INFORMAL CONTACTS WITHIN THE EUROPEAN UNION

For a civil servant working in a policy area with a European dimension, lobbying and information gathering have no beginning and no end – it should be a continuous, planned process whose focus shifts according to the state of play of a particular dossier.

Get in early. EU policies are like supertankers – a small nudge early on can make an enormous difference to the end position, but the later you leave it the harder you have to push to make any difference at all. Produce the first bit of paper, and then you will have set the agenda.

Maintain good personal contacts with Commission and other member state officials, relevant industry groups and other interested parties (consumer groups, NGOs etc.). Not only does this mean you'll have a better understanding of their position, but it will also increase the chances of you hearing about new developments in the policy area early on. If your contacts respect you, you will also be better placed to put your point of view across.

You should identify and build alliances with opposite numbers in other member states. (You should use UKRep and other embassies to help develop those alliances.) But don't just talk to 'friends' – after all, it is not them you need to convince.

Don't forget the European Parliament! This institution has a very important influence over the European agenda, with the vast majority of legislation jointly adopted by it and the Council. Identify the key MEPs in your policy area (UKRep can help a lot here) – often those on the relevant committee – and develop a relationship with them. Often, you can be one of their most reliable sources of information.

Effective lobbying is a two-way street. Always try to be able

to offer some information on others' positions or facts about
the issue at hand in exchange for what you want.

Get UK industry to make full use of Europe-wide trade associations in lobbying the Commission, and encourage them to
get their opposite numbers in other countries to seek support
from their national governments.

Consult interested parties in the UK. In addition to keeping them up to date with progress, the information they can
give you on likely effects will help inform both your lobbying
and your negotiating strategies and offer alternative ways of
achieving the same end. Consider all forms of consultation,
not just a formal paper document: focus groups, email lists,
websites, workshops, seminars etc.

It is often helpful to get other government departments
on your side. The Treasury can be particularly helpful, e.g. in
encouraging other finance ministries to object to another
country's attempt to subsidise (i.e. pay 'state aid' to) one of
its industries.

Do not forget to lobby cabinets as well as the Services: the
two operate fairly independently. UKRep will help you do this.

NEGOTIATING WITHIN THE
EUROPEAN UNION

Formal negotiation takes place first at a technical level in
Council working groups. Here, officials from all the member states and the Commission, chaired by the presidency,

seek to resolve as many of the issues as possible. When they have achieved all they can, the dossier will be passed up to COREPER (the Committee of Permanent Representatives) and then to ministers in the Council for final agreement (or referral back for more work).

Here are the key things you need to remember if you want to lead a successful negotiation:

- You should have a clear, prioritised strategy, agreed by ministers. Ideally this will have already informed your lobbying activities. Avoid taking up an inflexible negotiating position. Be clear about the outcomes you are trying to achieve, the areas of national interest that you want to promote and protect, and the principles you want to see applied. Develop some awareness of potential fall-back options and try to give your negotiators as much flexibility as possible. Be aware that under QMV it may not be possible to protect all your interests in a complex negotiation, meaning that there may be occasions when ministers decide to vote against a proposal. And keep close to the Cabinet Office at all stages of the negotiation, as the secretariat to the European Affairs Committee plays a key role.

- Ensure excellent communication between negotiators on the ground and the policy leads in London. They must never stray beyond the ministerially agreed mandate.

- You may not personally believe in European integration. But overt Euroscepticism can raise hackles in Brussels. However, this doesn't mean that the national interest doesn't matter. There is generally a great deal of willingness to accommodate particular national difficulties. Wherever possible, back up your arguments with facts – often obtained through national consultation.

- Be aware of the dynamic of the negotiation. The very beginning is usually the time for declarations of principle, but things move quickly into discussions of detail. As the process accelerates and the pressure to reach agreement grows, it becomes almost impossible to introduce new elements or to reopen points already agreed.

- Know when to give up on a point that is of little real importance. Multiple interventions on minor points of detail can quickly exhaust the patience of others around the table, and can often best be dealt with by a quiet word with the presidency or the General Secretariat.

- Try to keep a feel for that intangible but vital commodity, negotiating capital. Making concessions on items you have portrayed as important to you earns you capital. Winning a point (or even fighting it too hard) spends it.

- Aim to maintain your informal contacts and use them between formal sessions and, where appropriate, in the margins of those sessions too. Generally, the best way to garner support is to float an idea informally first, then, when you have secured sufficient support (usually involving the presidency and, if at all possible, the Commission), raise it in a formal session.

Don't forget that what you are negotiating is law. Keep close contact with your lawyers to make sure the text really does mean what you think it does. They can also help you keep in mind how the text before you will be turned into national law. Negotiation and transposition are not separate processes, and the need for fair but effective enforcement must be addressed whilst directives are being negotiated.

EUROPEAN UNION – STRUCTURE

The European Union was established as a legal entity in 2009 under the terms of the Treaty on the Functioning of the European Union (TFEU), otherwise known as the Lisbon Treaty.

Its predecessors were the European Economic Community, later renamed the European Community, which was established in 1958 by the Treaty of Paris. The European Union (the EU) was formed in 1992 by the Maastricht Treaty. It wasn't at first a legal entity, but instead consisted of three 'pillars':

- The two European Communities:

  (a) The European Atomic Energy Community;

  (b) The European Community (the EC).

- Common Foreign and Security Policy;

- Police and Judicial Co-operation.

The 2007 Lisbon Treaty, which came into force on 1 January 2010, abolished these three pillars.

There are two other key structures:

- Almost all member states (one of the exceptions being the UK) plus Iceland, Norway and Switzerland have removed all internal border controls (and are generally referred to as the Schengen area after the Convention that originally introduced this approach).

- A majority of member states (but again not including the UK) had by early 2011 entered into Economic and Monetary Union (EMU) and adopted the single currency (the Euro), on terms agreed in the Treaty of Maastricht in 1992. Member states joining the EU after 2011 are required to join the EMU.

Current membership of the Schengen area and EMU can be found online.

INSTITUTIONS

For most purposes, there are five main institutions that influence the Union in various ways:

- The Council of the European Union (the Council of Ministers);

- The European Parliament;

- The European Commission;

- The Court of Justice ('the ECJ');

- The Court of Auditors.

The Council of the European Union is, with the Parliament, one of the two main law-making and decision-making bodies in the EU. It is often referred to as the Council of Ministers and should not be confused with the Council of Europe, which was established after the Second World War with the aim of protecting Europe against totalitarianism.

The Council (usually together with the European Parliament) agrees legislation, budgets and other rules for most of the more familiar activities of the EU, such as the single market, and common policies like those on agriculture and fishing, environmental protection, trade and the free movement of goods, persons, services and money.

In addition, the Council is the main EU institution responsible for inter-governmental co-operation on common foreign and security policy (assisted by the High Representative for Common Foreign and Security Policy) and on justice and home affairs.

The Council brings together representatives of all the member state governments and is the forum in which these representatives assert their interests and reach compromises. These meetings happen regularly at a range of levels – expert officials from capitals, diplomats from the Permanent Representations (broadly speaking, member states' embassies), ministers and, at least four times a year, at the level of Presidents and Prime Ministers in the European Council. These 'summits' are chaired by the President of the European Council.

Ministerial Council meetings (Environment, Competitiveness, Agriculture etc.) take place between one and fifteen times a year, depending on the Council. Each meeting is attended by the appropriate minister from each member state (or their permanent representative) and the relevant Commissioner. The Council is chaired by a rotating presidency from amongst the member states (of which more below), changing every six months. Most of the work is done in the 300-plus working groups, which in turn feed into COREPER (the Committee of Permanent Representatives) and thence to ministers. The Council is also assisted by permanent staff called the General Secretariat of the Council, not to be confused with the Secretariat-General of the Commission – see further below.

The member state that holds the presidency of the Council has a key role, working closely as a 'trio' with its two successors. The trio sets long-term goals and prepares a common agenda determining the topics and major issues that will be addressed by the Council over an eighteen-month period. On the basis of this programme, each of the three countries prepares its own more detailed six-month programme. Note, by the way, that the presidency has the ability to stall progress in policy areas where it is in a minority.

Most Council decisions are taken by Qualified Majority Voting. Your departmental experts will be able to tell you the current definition of a 'qualified majority', including the number of votes currently available to be cast by each member state.

The European Parliament (EP), which usually shares decision-making with the Council, is made up of directly elected representatives from the member states, roughly in proportion to population. Most decisions are prepared in committees (usually in Brussels) and finally voted on in the regular plenary sessions (usually in Strasbourg).

The Parliament's principal roles are to:

· Examine and adopt European legislation. Most legislation is now agreed under the co-decision procedure, where Parliament shares power with the Council;

· Approve the EU budget;

· Exercise democratic control over the other EU institutions, for example by setting up committees of inquiry;

· Assent to important international agreements such as the accession of new EU member states and trade or association agreements between the EU and other countries.

As with national parliaments, the EP has specialist committees to deal with particular issues (foreign affairs, budget, environment and so on). Most of its work is in fact done through these committees.

It is well worth visiting the Parliament buildings in Brussels, if only to be astonished by their scale. There are also daily visits to the Parliament Chamber, with audio guides in the twenty-four (!)

official EU languages – details from the Infopoint at the west entrance to the central of the three Parliament buildings.

The European Commission is headed by twenty-eight senior figures, one from each of the member states, but formally (and very often actually) independent of national allegiance, making up the College of Commissioners. Each has a small group of officials – their Cabinet – to assist them to monitor and drive the development of policy. The President of the Commission usually chairs the College's weekly meetings. A staff of about 33,000 – divided between around thirty-six directorates-general and Services (including the Secretariat-General, press and translation service) – support the College.

The European Commission does much of the day-to-day work in the European Union. In most areas of EU business it is the only body that can draft proposals for new legislation, which it presents to the European Parliament and the Council. The Commission makes sure that EU decisions are properly implemented and supervises the way EU funds are spent. It is also charged with ensuring that everyone abides by the European treaties and European law. With the major exception of competition policy, it doesn't generally have a large role in implementation or enforcement on the ground – this is primarily a member state responsibility. In certain areas (see the section on competence), the Commission also has the role of representing the EU in external (i.e. with non-EU countries) negotiations and meetings.

The Court of Justice of the European Union is the final arbiter of all questions of European law. The CJEU (also often referred to as the ECJ – its previous name) ensures the consistent and accurate interpretation of European law across the EU. If national courts are in doubt about how to apply EU rules they must ask the Court of Justice. Member states, certain EU institutions and individuals can also bring proceedings against EU institutions before the Court. Some less significant cases can also be heard by its subsidiary court, the General Court. The CJEU consists of one independent judge from each EU country.

The court sits in Luxembourg, and you must take care not to confuse it with the non-EU bodies the European Court of Human Rights in Strasbourg and the International Court of Justice in The Hague.

The European Court of Auditors, also located in Luxembourg, is the body that checks how EU money is spent, both directly by other institutions and, where appropriate, by member states (for example agricultural subsidies or regional development aid).

These five key institutions are flanked by five other bodies of varying importance:

- The European Central Bank (responsible for monetary policy and managing the euro);

- The Economic and Social Committee (expresses the opinions of organised civil society on economic and social issues);

- The Committee of the Regions (expresses the opinions of regional and local authorities);

- The Ombudsman (deals with citizens' complaints about maladministration by any EU institution or body);

- The European Investment Bank (helps achieve EU objectives by financing investment projects).

A large number of agencies (such as the European Medicines Evaluation Agency, European Food Safety Authority and so on) and other bodies complete the system.

EUROPEAN UNION LEGISLATION

The primary legislation of the EU is in the treaties themselves. These provide for the adoption of five kinds of 'act'.

- Opinions and Recommendations are non-binding guidance.

- Decisions are binding in their entirety upon those to whom they are addressed (individuals, companies, countries).

- Regulations are binding in their entirety and are generally and directly applicable in all member states.

- Directives set out the result to be achieved but leave the choice of form and methods to the national authorities in each member state to which they are addressed – in other words, they always require transposition into national law.

Co-decision

Most EU legislation is adopted through a process called co-decision. This can be a very complex procedure, but the basic outline is given below. Be careful, though – this is a simplified description and there can be many twists and turns on the road, and some steps may happen more or less at the same time. In addition, if all parties agree, the process can be stopped at any point after the European Parliament's First Reading and the proposal adopted. Indeed, huge attempts are in practice made to get agreement at the first reading stage, which necessitates an informal institutional negotiation called a 'trilogue'.

- The Commission makes a proposal for legislation to the EP and the Council.

- The EP gives its First Reading opinion on the proposal, in the form of a series of amendments. (Note that the opinion is adopted on the basis of a simple majority of MEPs voting in the plenary session.)

- The Commission gives its views on the EP's amendments and changes its proposal accordingly.

- The Council adopts its Common Position, taking into consideration the EP's amendments.

The voting is usually by Qualified Majority (though sometimes

unanimity applies throughout) if the Commission con-
curs; otherwise unanimity is needed. The Commission then
forwards the Common Position to the EP, along with an explanation of its reasons.

- The EP then has three months to examine the Common Position,
  along with the Commission's views on it. Within this period
  it adopts its Second Reading amendments. This time only
  amendments achieving the support of an absolute majority of
  MEPs (that is, half of all MEPs plus one) go through.

- The Council now has three months to decide which of the EP
  amendments it will take on board. The Council can usually adopt
  those amendments on which the Commission has expressed a
  positive opinion by QMV (though sometimes unanimity applies
  throughout), but the Council needs unanimity for those where the
  Commission has expressed a negative opinion. If all amendments
  are accepted, the process ends and the proposal is adopted.

- If one or more amendments are rejected, then conciliation starts.
  The Conciliation Committee must meet within six weeks of the
  rejection and reach a conclusion within a further six weeks. It is
  made up of representatives of the member states (usually chaired
  by a minister, with other member states represented by the
  Permanent Representative or his deputy) plus an equal number of
  MEPs. The Commission is tasked with assisting the Committee.

- If conciliation is successful, the Council (QMV or sometimes

unanimity) and the EP (absolute majority) must each then adopt
the modified text within another six weeks.

Comitology

Once legislation has been agreed, there will often be an ongoing
need to update it to account for technical progress/changes, to
oversee its implementation and to draw up guidance. This is
generally done by the Commission, assisted (or interfered with,
depending on your point of view) by a committee made up of
representatives of the member states. This goes by the delight-
fully uninformative name of comitology and can have significant
effects on policy in the UK. Although these are technical committees, it is important that you understand when the stakes
are high – for instance for UK manufacturing and jobs, or for
the environment – and you might need to send more senior
representatives in order to maximise the chances of a good outcome for the UK. UKRep can provide very helpful assistance and
advice if you alert them to the significance of the negotiation.

IMPLICATIONS FOR THE UK

Competence

The first key question you need to ask when working on EU
issues is whether or not there is EU competence in this policy area. This is the jargon phrase for whether or not the EU

already has a role/responsibility in a particular area, and if so how much of one.

Some areas are of exclusive competence for the EU: the EU is the only body with the right to develop policy in this area and the Commission speaks for the EU. The best examples here are agriculture and international trade. One good (but alas not definitive) clue is if people talk about a 'Common XXX Policy'.

Other areas of policy are of mixed competence for the EU: it has a significant role, but so do the member states and they can speak for themselves in international discussions. Good examples include environmental policy and development aid.

The third category, logically, is that of national competence, where the EU has no significant role (often being limited to information exchange, exhortation and so on). Examples here are military matters, healthcare provision and education. It is also true to say that there is a tendency over time for the EU to try to extend its competence – to transform mixed competence into exclusive, and national competence into mixed.

In attempting to answer the competence question, you must remember that even in the areas of pure national competence there can be overspill. Just because you are commissioning a brand new hospital (healthcare provision), it doesn't mean you can ignore EU rules on public procurement or state aids. If there is exclusive EU competence, then the probable implication is that you cannot do anything at a national level that has a legal effect, and even some exhortation or tax/spend options may not be feasible. Your main option in this instance is to try to persuade the EU to act as you would like, which has its own problems and risks.

If there is mixed competence then you will probably need more expert advice on whether there is a conflict or not, usually from your lawyers. If there is no conflict, or only national competence, and there is no overspill, then off you go! However, you may wish to consider checking with the Commission to ensure it also agrees there is no problem (it'll probably find out about the policy sooner or later – many Commission officials regularly listen to the *Today* programme and read the *Financial Times* – so it's best to make sure there won't be problems down the line). You may also want to keep the Commission and/or other member states informed of what you are doing, especially if you might be able to learn something from their experience or if you might at some stage want to export your ideas to the European level.

Other typical EU issues that may have implications for national policy are:

- Transposition/gold-plating: This issue is considered in the previous chapter.

- Environmental impact: There are rules on carrying out environmental impact assessments on a range of projects.

- Subsidies: Public authorities may not provide support in cash or kind to someone in a way, or for a purpose, that runs counter to the rules on state aids.

- Public procurement (purchasing goods and services by the state, broadly defined): There are some strict rules which require the state to ensure that companies from other member states are able to find out about, and tender for, significant public procurement on an equal basis.

- Free movement of goods, services, labour and capital: There is a general prohibition on establishing legal or practical barriers to these 'four freedoms' without good reason, such as public security, or protection of the environment. In some areas, failure to notify such barriers to the Commission can result in them being invalid and unenforceable in the courts. (This follows a case in the Netherlands where failure to notify technical standards for supply of breathalysers resulted in all who had been convicted of drink driving on the basis of tests by those breathalysers having their convictions quashed!)

- Competition law: Deliberately or accidentally putting up barriers to competition.

Your department will have experts who can guide you in all of these areas. Your role is to get in touch with them early, before you make any mistakes!

EUROPEAN UNION: KEY DATES

1952 – Treaty of Paris (1951) between six countries – Belgium, France, Germany, Italy, Luxembourg and the Netherlands – enters into force. European Coal and Steel Community (ECSC) created.

1958 – Treaties of Rome (1957) enter into force. European Atomic Energy Community (Euratom) and European Economic Community (EEC – later renamed the EC) created.

1973 – Denmark, Ireland and the UK join the communities, bringing the total to nine.

1981 – Greece joins.

1986 – Portugal and Spain join, bringing the total to twelve.

1987 – Single European Act (1986) enters into force.

1993 – Maastricht Treaty (1992) enters into force. EU created.

1993 – Single market 'completed'.

1995 – Austria, Finland and Sweden join the EU, bringing the total to fifteen.

1999 – Amsterdam Treaty (1997) enters into force.

1999 – Economic and Monetary Union starts.

2000 – Pre-enlargement Inter-Governmental Conference
(IGC) starts.

2002 – Treaty of Paris (and hence the ECSC) expires.

2002 – Introduction of Euro coins and notes.

2004 – Enlargement: Cyprus, Czech Republic, Estonia,
Hungary, Latvia, Lithuania, Malta, Poland,
Slovakia and Slovenia all join, bringing the total
to twenty-five.

2007 – Bulgaria and Romania join, bringing the total to
twenty-seven.

2009 – The Lisbon Treaty (Treaty on the Functioning of
the European Union – TFEU) comes into force.
European Community and European Atomic
Energy Community abolished.

2013 – Croatia joins, bringing the total to twenty-eight.

Chapter 5

Civil Service Ethics

C IVIL SERVANTS WORK within a wide range of
ethical and other constraints that are taken very
seriously by both senior staff and the wider public. One of our key skills, therefore, is to achieve
our objectives whilst observing both the letter and the spirit
of our various obligations.

To begin at the beginning, we work within a constitutional
framework known as the Westminster model, which in particular requires us to be both politically impartial and principally
accountable only to ministers within the current government. This
is to some extent codified in the Civil Service Code, summarised
in greater detail below. Subsequent parts of this chapter look at:

- Integrity, conflicts of interest and financial interests;

- Impartiality;

- Political impartiality;

- Recruitment and promotion;

- Judicial review – including the obligation to obey all laws;

- Human rights;

- Transparency and Freedom of Information;

- Data protection;

- The acceptance of sponsorship by the private sector.

THE CIVIL SERVICE CODE

The Civil Service Code summarises the constitutional and ethical framework within which all civil servants work. Its introduction reads as follows:

> The civil service is an integral and key part of the government of the United Kingdom. It supports the government of the day in developing and implementing its policies, and in delivering public services.

Civil servants are accountable to ministers, who in turn are accountable to Parliament.

As a civil servant, you are appointed on merit on the basis of fair and open competition and are expected to carry out your role with dedication and a commitment to the civil service and its core values: integrity, honesty, objectivity and impartiality.

In this code:

- 'integrity' is putting the obligations of public service above your own personal interests;

- 'honesty' is being truthful and open;

- 'objectivity' is basing your advice and decisions on rigorous analysis of the evidence; and

- 'impartiality' is acting solely according to the merits of the case and serving equally well governments of different political persuasions.

These core values support good government and ensure the achievement of the highest possible standards in all that the civil service does. This in turn helps the civil service to gain and retain the respect of ministers, Parliament, the public and its customers.

The requirements of honesty and objectivity are fairly straightforward. On honesty, the code says that:

You must: set out the facts and relevant issues truthfully, and correct

any errors as soon as possible; and use resources only for the authorised public purposes for which they are provided.

You must not: deceive or knowingly mislead ministers, Parliament
or others; or be influenced by improper pressures from others or the
prospect of personal gain.

On objectivity, the code says that:

You must: provide information and advice, including advice to ministers, on the basis of the evidence, and accurately present the options
and facts; take decisions on the merits of the case; and take due
account of expert and professional advice.

You must not: ignore inconvenient facts or relevant considerations when providing advice or making decisions; or frustrate the
implementation of policies once decisions are taken by declining to
take, or abstaining from, action which flows from those decisions.

The integrity and impartiality requirements are a little more
subtle and discussed in more detail below.

INTEGRITY

The Civil Service Code says that:

You must:

• fulfil your duties and obligations responsibly;

- always act in a way that is professional and that deserves and retains the confidence of all those with whom you have dealings;

- carry out your fiduciary obligations responsibly (that is, make sure public money and other resources are used properly and efficiently);

- deal with the public and their affairs fairly, efficiently, promptly, effectively and sensitively, to the best of your ability;

- keep accurate official records and handle information as openly as possible within the legal framework; and

- comply with the law and uphold the administration of justice.

You must not:

- misuse your official position, for example by using information acquired in the course of your official duties to further your private interests or those of others;

- accept gifts or hospitality or receive other benefits from anyone which might reasonably be seen to compromise your personal judgement or integrity; or

- disclose official information without authority. This duty continues to apply after you leave the civil service.

Conflicts of Interest

Great care needs to be taken to avoid conflicts of interest, whether real or perceived. You may be certain that you could rise above them, but others will doubt it. All potential conflicts of interest, including conflicts with the interests of your immediate family, must therefore be disclosed to managers, remembering that an innocuous friendship, investment, gift or treat can be transformed overnight into a possible conflict of interest. The following paragraphs provide guidance, but nothing in them should be taken to detract from departmental guidance, which should be consulted, and taken to prevail, in case of doubt. Indeed, certain individual departments, or parts of departments, have additional requirements above those mentioned below.

Gifts, Hospitality Etc.

These may be divided into three categories.

First, there are gifts from a company whose services you are using or might use, or with whom you might negotiate grants or other support, or which might materially benefit from decisions with which you might be involved. There are absolutely no circumstances in which you can accept a gift of any value, or any hospitality more substantial than a working lunch, from such a source. This prohibition extends to the use of air miles and other benefits offered by the travel trade etc.

Second, expensive gifts (each department defines its own

limit) from other donors must also generally be refused or returned. Alternatively, it is sometimes possible to say to the donor, 'Thank you for the gift, which I will use in the office rather than for my personal use.' (You can donate wine to the Christmas party.) Failing this, you can hand the gift over to the department, or pay the department to let you keep it.

Third, any gifts, hospitality etc. whose acceptance is not prohibited under the first two rules above should also be refused unless the acceptance can clearly be justified as contributing to the achievement of your objectives. Put another way, the reason for the acceptance has to be clearly defensible, always remembering the Greek proverb that 'gifts are poison'.

Positive reasons for accepting hospitality include the need to carry out an ambassadorial role, make contacts and gain information. It is therefore generally OK to attend celebrations of a company's success or longevity, or an industry-wide gathering, including trade association dinners. It is also reasonable to accept inexpensive gifts such as ties and pens, so as to avoid giving offence. Conversely, it is important to avoid developing a sense of obligation to a host or donor, and to avoid criticism (from those unable to benefit) of benefiting from lavish hospitality etc. In general, therefore, you should not accept tickets for major sporting events, Glyndebourne or Covent Garden. It is seldom a good argument that you are establishing or maintaining contacts at such events, because it is seldom appropriate or possible to discuss business. It is often useful to apply the 'wow' test. When you receive an invitation and find yourself saying 'wow' then it is time to refuse.

A similar approach should be adopted when considering whether you might be accompanied by a partner to an event. Indeed, the negative factors can be more intense, given that the cost to the host will have doubled, and the opportunity to do business will have diminished. On the other hand, it can be helpful to be accompanied by a partner to an event at which one is trying to build up a relationship with the host or to an event at which one is acting as an ambassador, for instance at a company celebration or an event in aid of charity.

It is usually OK to accept local transport, lunch and refreshments when visiting private sector companies. But you may never let a private sector company pay your rail fare, air fare or overnight hotel bill. It is also acceptable to accept overnight accommodation in a company's guest house provided for that purpose, but of course you must not then claim overnight subsistence. And it is permissible to accept a free flight in a company plane if there is no convenient public transport and if the plane would have been making the journey anyway. But the offer of such transport should be refused if convenient public transport is available, or if the provision of the flight would cause the company to incur significant expense.

Financial Interests

We must all take particular care to avoid profiting, or enabling others to profit (or even getting into a position where we could do these things) from information which is supplied to us in confidence. In particular, you must consult your line manager if you are asked to handle papers concerning any company (including a bank) in which you have invested, or with which you have any financial link. (However, standard bank accounts may be ignored for this purpose, unless they contain a huge amount of money.) You must also tell your manager if you hold shares in, or have any other link with, any company that is dealt with by you or your colleagues. You must do this immediately on joining the team, or immediately on acquiring the shares etc. This applies even if the shares are held via a PEP or ISA. Holdings in collective vehicles such as OEICs and unit trusts need not be reported unless you have a large holding (over £1,000) and you know that your trust has invested in a company or companies with which you are dealing.

You must also tell your line manager about any other employment or self-employment. And you must disclose links to all other bodies (including charities) if it looks as though you might be asked to deal with them on behalf of the department.

There are also strict rules about business appointments after retirement. It is obviously important that there should be no cause for any suspicion of impropriety when you take up a new job after retirement. All offers of employment should therefore be reported to your department, who will if necessary involve the Advisory Committee on Business Appointments, which gives advice on applications at the most senior levels, and reviews a wider sample in order to ensure consistency and effectiveness.

IMPARTIALITY

The Civil Service Code says that:

> You must: carry out your responsibilities in a way that is fair, just
> and equitable and reflects the civil service commitment to equality
> and diversity.
>
> You must not: act in a way that unjustifiably favours or discrimi-
> nates against particular individuals or interests.

The public accordingly expect both ministers and their officials
to deal equally with everyone, and with every organisation,
without prejudice, favour or disfavour. This simple but vital
concept has a number of useful consequences.

First, it enables you to ask appropriate questions, however
grand the person or organisation with which you are dealing.
For instance, an inquiry into the financial standing of a multi-
national can often be less rigorous than a similar inquiry of a
small firm. But large firms and substantial charities can go bust
(remember Kids Company), so you should never take anything
for granted. Ask a carefully targeted question and then decide
whether further questions are necessary. Take particular care
if you have heard a critical rumour or comment. There can be
smoke without fire, but the two are usually closely associated.

Second, it is your defence against the senior or public figure
who might otherwise expect you to give them priority, or rubber-
stamp some sort of application. You must never allow queue
jumping, nor must you ever refrain from asking a pertinent

question, whoever you are dealing with. (It is of course perfectly reasonable to 'fast track' some work for a senior person who has a genuine need for it to be done quickly. But you must be sure that you would do the same for anyone else with a similar need, and that they are not jumping ahead of someone whose needs are just as great but who is less well connected.)

Incidentally, the vast majority of senior/public figures understand perfectly well that they have to receive the same treatment as everyone else. If they get stroppy then (a) they believe that everyone should be receiving better treatment (if they are right then you should improve the service to everyone), or (b) they are trying to hide something (never allow yourself to be bullied into dropping a potentially important line of questioning), or (c) they are simply pompous (in which case don't favour them, but don't set out to punish them either).

Third, it is your defence against anyone, including journalists, who might ask you to give them advice and information that you have not given to others. If possible, of course, you should be free with information. But there are no circumstances in which you should give information or advice to one person that you would not give to anyone else who asked a similar question.

POLITICAL IMPARTIALITY

The Civil Service Code says the following on the need for political impartiality:

You must:

- serve the government, whatever its political persuasion,
  to the best of your ability in a way which maintains political
  impartiality and is in line with the requirements of this code,
  no matter what your own political beliefs are;

- act in a way which deserves and retains the confidence of
  ministers, whilst at the same time ensuring that you will be able
  to establish the same relationship with those whom you may
  be required to serve in some future government; and

- comply with any restrictions that have been laid down on
  your political activities.

You must not:

- act in a way that is determined by party political considerations; or

- use official resources for party political purposes; or

- allow your personal political views to determine any advice you
  give or your actions.

Let me add some detail:

The civil service is required to be politically impartial, and
to be able loyally and with equal commitment to serve governments of all political persuasions. This means that:

- You may not publicly defend the decisions and views of your ministers (as distinct from explaining them), including in social and other media, or by writing to newspapers;

- You must even avoid saying or writing anything which could be quoted as demonstrating that you personally (or your colleagues) either agree or disagree with ministers' decisions;

- You may not disclose the advice that you have given to ministers.

But on the other hand:

- You must explain and implement your ministers' policies with real commitment, whatever your personal views.

It can be very hard to follow the above advice, especially when a minister or special adviser does not share your view of the border line between 'explaining' a policy and 'defending' it. It is even more difficult if you strongly support – or strongly object to – decisions that have been made, or might be made, by ministers. It is not always possible to hide those views from colleagues, and it is sometimes difficult to hide them from those outside the government with whom you come into frequent contact. But it is absolutely essential that you give no sign that you oppose the principles and underlying thrust of the government's policies, nor must you suggest that you do not respect your minister.

It can be even more difficult to follow the above advice

where minor decisions are concerned. ('Of course I will try to get him to open your conference. It's an important occasion.') But you will learn from bitter experience that the advice is sensible, for it is embarrassing all round when the minister refuses to do what you suggest. There is, I am afraid, no alternative to sounding rather pathetic and merely promising that the case will be put to the minister, adding that you cannot predict the result. Quite simply, it should never be possible for anyone to be able to criticise ministers for failing to take your advice. And it is even more important that incoming ministers should be unaware of the extent or otherwise of your personal support for their predecessors' policies.

Equally, you may not be asked to engage in activities which call into question your political impartiality, or which give rise to criticism that people paid from public funds are being used for party political purposes. You may not, of course, engage in political activities. And you may not help draft 'Dear Colleague' letters unless they are to be sent to all MPs. You are, however, allowed to provide ministers with facts that might be used in political speeches etc., and you are allowed to check ministers' political speeches for factual accuracy. You are also allowed to comment on the analysis, costings and proposals contained in documents produced by political organisations, including the opposition, but you must not draft ministers' responses to such documents.

You may not brief an MP (including from the government party) or agree that an MP may visit a government office etc. without ministerial approval. Ministers will usually agree to factual or uncontroversial briefings and visits, but they sometimes want to get involved themselves, in which case any meeting or visit has to be arranged at a time convenient for both the minister and the MP.

For the avoidance of doubt, however, you are expected to take politics into account when giving advice to ministers. You are employed to help ministers achieve their objectives and this means being aware of, and respectful of the substance of, likely attacks from the opposition benches, the House of Lords and hostile media. Then, once ministers have made their decisions, you are expected to help them defend their policies even if you don't agree with them. Minister Nick Harvey put it very well when he said: 'I was not looking for politically biased advice but I did want advice that was politically aware: political neutrality was fine, but political naivety was unhelpful.'

RECRUITMENT AND PROMOTION

The Civil Service Code says that civil servants must be appointed on merit on the basis of fair and open competition. The following notes provide additional practical advice in this area.

The Basic Rules

It is fairly straightforward to arrange a level transfer (i.e. without a significant pay rise) of an official from one job to another. But the need to avoid nepotism and favouritism means that you need to take great care when appointing someone from outside the civil service, or promoting someone from within it. The basic rules for these appointments are as follows.

- All such appointments must be made on the basis of fair and open competition.

- All prospective applicants must be given equal and reasonable access to adequate information about the job and its requirements, and about the selection process.

- All applicants must be considered equally on merit at each stage of the selection process.

- Selection must be based on relevant criteria applied consistently to all the candidates.

- Selection techniques must be reliable and guard against bias.

You cannot therefore appoint someone to a job without an advertisement and competition, even if you believe them to be ideally or uniquely suitable. There are limited exceptions, such as for temporary appointments and inward secondees, but you should take a close look at the relevant guidance before attempting to make use of such exceptions.

JUDICIAL REVIEW

It almost goes without saying that the government itself, and individual civil servants, must take particular care to obey the law. After all, if the lawmakers and their servants will not respect the law, why should anyone else? It follows that it is a very serious matter for an individual civil servant to be dishonest, whether in their private or their public life.

It is equally important that we apply the utmost good faith in our official dealings with the judicial machine. If we become involved in a legal dispute, we have a duty to assist the court by drawing all appropriate facts, documents and arguments to its attention. There can be no question of hiding or distorting evidence so as to improve the chances of 'success', even if it is felt that such tactics are being deployed by the other side.

Unlike the private sector, we are also subject to judge-made 'administrative law' in the form of judicial review (JR) of decisions made by public bodies, including the government. As one judge put it: 'Judicial review is about telling the powerful how to behave when they make decisions.'

There is excellent official guidance in a booklet entitled 'The Judge Over Your Shoulder'. And the first four sentences usually make quite an impact on those who read about JR for the first time:

> You are sitting at your desk granting licences on behalf of your minister. Your enabling statutory powers are in the widest possible terms: 'The Secretary of State may grant licences on such conditions as he

thinks fit.' With power like that you might think that there could be no possible ground for legal challenge in the courts whatever you do. But you would be wrong.

This is a very dynamic part of the law, and decisions are greatly influenced by the judge's perception of whether the powerful have acted fairly (a very subjective concept) in all the circumstances. It is in particular strongly influenced by human rights considerations. Every civil servant should therefore read 'The Judge Over Your Shoulder'. And you should also consult a lawyer before you, or your minister, make any decision that might conceivably be challenged as being in some way unfair.

The following extracts from a 2014 Supreme Court judgment give a flavour of how the law has developed over the years:

> The courts … have developed an issue-sensitive scale of intervention to enable them to perform their constitutional function in an increasingly complex polity. They continue to abstain from merits review – in effect, retaking the decision on the facts – but in appropriate classes of case they will today look very closely at the process by which facts have been ascertained and at the logic of the inferences drawn from them.
>
> The common law no longer insists on the uniform application of the rigid test of irrationality once thought applicable under the so-called Wednesbury principle. The nature of judicial review in every case depends upon the context … 'The court must … be entitled to subject an administrative decision to the more rigorous examination, to ensure that it is in no way flawed, according to the gravity of the issue which the decision determines.'

A further factor relevant to the intensity of review is whether the issue before the tribunal is one properly within the province of the court. As has often been said, judges are not 'equipped by training or experience or furnished with the requisite knowledge or advice' to decide issues depending on administrative or political judgment ... On the other hand, where the question is the fairness of a procedure adopted by a decision-maker, the court has been more willing to intervene: such questions are to be answered not by reference to Wednesbury unreasonableness, but 'in accordance with the principles of fair procedure which have been developed over the years and of which the courts are the author and sole judge'.

The Wednesbury test, by the way, requires the courts to intervene 'if no reasonable minister properly directing himself could have reached the impugned decision'. As noted above, this appears to be a stiff test, but decisions are in practice quashed more often than you would expect. So it is well worth stopping and considering whether your actions will appear fair and reasonable to a dispassionate observer well after the event.

And even if JR were 'merely' all about process, it is nevertheless true that good process will greatly increase the chances of your making a good decision, so JR has value if it persuades you not to cut corners. In addition, however, JR may be brought if there is any appearance of bias, or going beyond parliamentary authority.

Many applicants for judicial review claim that a minister has taken 'irrelevant factors' into account when making a decision. Of course many decisions are essentially political in nature, e.g. the balance to be struck between the needs of the environment and the needs of the economy. Parliament has therefore provided that such decisions must ultimately be taken by or on behalf of ministers. And ministers are politicians, not judges. They are therefore expected, and allowed, to make those decisions against the backdrop of their political agenda. But they are not expected, or allowed, to make decisions in a way that is limited by that agenda. Therefore, when advising ministers in these cases, you should divide the factors bearing on the decision into three classes:

(a) The first are those factors that are specified, in the appropriate legislation, as relevant to the decision. The decision has to be consistent with those factors. In other words, it should be possible to imagine a reasonable person taking a similar decision on the basis of the same facts, without taking into account other factors.

(b) Ministers may also take other relevant factors into account, such as the economic needs of a particular region, or the need to be seen to be encouraging competition.

(c) But ministers may not take into account irrelevant factors such as the regional political situation, or recent political donations from the company in question.

The border line between the categories can sometimes be indistinct. Can a minister take account of the special economic needs of his or her constituency? Legal advice should be taken if you are in any doubt.

HUMAN RIGHTS

It is important to be aware of the European (not EU) background to human rights legislation, which is now an intrinsic part of UK administrative law. The Human Rights Act 1998 incorporates the European Convention on Human Rights into UK law. The Convention is a treaty of the Council of Europe, which is based, along with the European Court of Human Rights, in Strasbourg. Neither body is part of the EU. The Convention guarantees a number of rights and freedoms, including:

- The right to a fair and public trial within a reasonable time (this applies to any case involving civil rights and obligations, and not just criminal trials);

- The right to respect for private and family life, home and correspondence; and

- The right to peaceful enjoyment of possessions and protection of property.

The Convention is intended, amongst other things, to promote the ideals and values of a democratic society. It is therefore to be given a broad and generous interpretation, and the courts will look at the substance and reality of what is involved, and not just the form. The Convention is also a dynamic document that must be interpreted in the light of present-day conditions. Societies and values change, and these changes are taken into account.

The Convention incorporates two important concepts. The first is proportionality – any interference with a Convention right must be in proportion to the aim being pursued. The second concept is legal certainty. Any action impinging on a human right must be authorised by a specific legal rule or regime and not, for instance, by non-statutory guidance.

The Strasbourg Court is supposed to be reluctant to substitute its own views for those of individual governments where the latter have tried to strike a balance between competing considerations, for instance between the needs of the community – to build a new railway, say – and individual property rights. Nevertheless, the Court has been very reluctant to permit, for example, the deprivation of property without compensation.

Turning to the UK legislation, it is already clear that the Human Rights Act has fundamentally altered the way in which the British courts approach the interpretation of statutory provisions. British judges need not slavishly follow European Court decisions, but they must take them into account. They will therefore seek to interpret UK legislation in a way that is compatible with the Convention. In doing so, the courts can quash or ignore secondary legislation, but they cannot override the clear meaning of primary legislation, even though it may be equally clear that the legislation is incompatible with the Convention. The courts will in these circumstances issue a declaration of incompatibility, whereupon Parliament must decide whether it agrees with the courts, and change the law, or whether it disagrees with the courts, and risk having the aggrieved citizen take the case to the European Court of Human Rights.

Even today, most civil servants outside the Home Office and the Department of Justice will seldom have to concern themselves with the majority of the provisions of the Act. Most of us are seldom in the business of removing the right to life, or to marry. But we do need to bear in mind that *the right to a fair trial* applies just as much to civil proceedings and tribunals as to the criminal law. Great care nowadays needs therefore to be taken to ensure that:

- Tribunals are genuinely independent and impartial – not political appointees and not on short-term appointments;

- Hearings are arranged reasonably quickly, and held in public, either initially or on appeal; and

- There are effective appeal provisions throughout the legislation for which we are responsible.

The RightsInfo website has lots of useful, easily accessible further information – and then, as ever, read your department's detailed guidance and take legal advice if you are unsure, or are challenged.

TRANSPARENCY AND FREEDOM
OF INFORMATION (FOI)

Civil servants working on the development of particular policies are not directly accountable to the public. We are accountable to ministers, who are in turn accountable to Parliament. But the public are our ultimate paymasters and we should therefore be open with them, unless there is a very good reason not to be. After all, we deal with complex issues and have no monopoly of wisdom or knowledge. It therefore makes sense to explain the way in which the government's policies are developing, before they are set in concrete, so that we can be told if we are getting anything wrong, and in particular if our assumptions are incorrect. We should also explain the way in which we administer our schemes and make decisions, and we should make available the internal guidance and rules that govern our procedures.

Ministers and officials have always argued that there should be two important constraints on transparency. First, we have respected the needs of those who have provided us with information in confidence, or with commercially sensitive information. We should not disclose such information without the permission of the person who provided it. Second, we have not disclosed our advice to ministers, for this weakens their position if they decide that they will not accept our advice. Open government in this area would thus tend to increase the power of officials as compared with ministers, and this is hardly in the interests of democracy. Similarly, there is a strict prohibition against revealing that the law officers have been consulted, let alone what they have advised.

The Supreme Court has summarised the competing pressures in this way:

> Information is the key to sound decision-making, to accountability and development; it underpins democracy and assists in combatting poverty, oppression, corruption, prejudice and inefficiency. Administrators, judges, arbitrators, and persons conducting inquiries and investigations depend upon it; likewise the press, NGOs and individuals concerned to report on issues of public interest. Unwillingness to disclose information may arise through habits of secrecy or reasons of self-protection. But information can be genuinely private, confidential or sensitive, and these interests merit respect in their own right and, in the case of those who depend on information to fulfil their functions, because this may not otherwise be forthcoming. These competing considerations, and the balance between them, lie behind the issues on this appeal.

Before the Freedom of Information Act came into force, if I was not sure whether to provide information, I asked myself whether we would provide it in response to a Parliamentary Question. If we would, then we should be prepared to give it without such a stimulus. But if we would refuse information to an MP, we should prima facie refuse to give it to the public. I rather doubt that the FoI Act has in practice moved the border line between what information should and should not be disclosed, although it has certainly strengthened the public's hand against ministers and officials who might have been tempted to be unduly secretive.

The FoI Act generally follows the approach described above, and establishes a general right of access to information held by public bodies, subject to certain exemptions. Some exemptions are absolute but most of the exemptions are qualified – that is, subject to a balancing 'public interest' test in which the public interest in secrecy needs to be balanced against the public interest in disclosure arising from benefits related to:

- Accountability and transparency;

- Greater understanding and public debate; and

- Allowing individuals to understand and challenge decisions.

Such qualified exemptions include:

- Personal information: see the separate discussion of data protection;

- Information relating to the formulation or development of government policy;

- Ministerial communications;

- Advice from the law officers – and requests for such advice;

- Information whose disclosure would be likely to prejudice collective responsibility;

- Information whose disclosure would constitute a breach of confidence; and

- Information whose disclosure would be likely to prejudice commercial interests.

Appeals against officials' decisions can be made to the Information Commissioner, who seems to be taking a pretty sensible line. One interesting decision was made in April 2007, when he forced the publication of advice to then Chancellor Gordon Brown on the likely consequences of changing the taxation of pension funds. The Commissioner recognised the 'chilling effect' associated with the publication of civil service advice, but also recognised that this effect should decline over time, and thought that, as the advice had been given ten years earlier, the balance had swung in favour of disclosure. There were clearly going to be plenty more appeals in this area, but it did begin to look as if the Commissioner would generally protect the confidentiality of officials' advice for some years, though there would need to be good reasons if he is to be persuaded that this period should exceed ten years.

More generally, however, if your default approach is to be open, and to respond positively to informal requests, then you will seldom if ever find yourself corresponding with the Information Commissioner. But if you seem to be getting into a dispute in this area then make sure that you read the Act and the guidance material very carefully, and also consult experienced colleagues, including your department's Freedom of Information officer. There is also some very helpful advice on the website of the Information Commissioner. But do bear in mind that, if you assert the need for confidentiality and are overruled, the public are more likely to see conspiracy than cock-up.

DATA PROTECTION

Like human rights law, data protection legislation is firmly based on a European law, but this time it is based on a very old and poorly drafted (or at least very dated and highly bureaucratic) EU directive, which was itself based on 1950s German legislation reacting to the excesses of the period of Nazi government. The directive, and hence our legislation, accordingly seeks to protect people, rather than protect data, and so is hard to enforce in these days of electronic data etc.

There are two aspects to this legislation.

The first is the accessibility of personal data to those interested in knowing what has been said and written about them. This applies particularly to employees, including fellow civil servants.

The second is the protection of personal data in general, and by extension the data held on IT systems.

The first and primary aspect of the data protection regime is the more troublesome, given our political masters' natural

tendency to be less than wholly frank with the public and our
staff. The law is complex, but it is best to work on the basis
that the public and our staff are entitled to know what has been
written about them. References provided 'in confidence', for
instance, need not be disclosed to the subject by the writer,
but the subject can approach the person who received the reference, who then needs to judge whether 'it is reasonable in
all the circumstances' to disclose it. As with FoI, therefore,
the best approach is to be prepared to disclose information
and honest views about individuals to those individuals (but
to no one else) – but take advice if you believe that this would
be unwise. Also, as with FoI, you might do a lot worse than
to start by reading the very helpful good-practice notes on the
Information Commissioner's website.

Following the events of early 2008, when HMRC lost two
discs containing detailed information about all child benefit
claimants, there can hardly be anyone in government who is
not acutely aware of the second aspect of the legislation, and
the need to put a lot of effort into protecting personal data.
Put crudely, it needs to be protected just as well as we protect
money. Just as you need to learn and comply with the rules
that limit the scope for financial fraud so you need to learn and
comply with your department's rules requiring the encryption,
safe transmission etc. of personal data. If you are handling
any form of such data, and don't understand the rules, then
you must ask.

Finally, two general points. Data protection legislation
trumps FoI legislation, so that you cannot, for instance,

provide personal information about an individual, including an employee, in response to an FoI request.

But the legislation does not stop you providing personal information to another authority when it is clearly in the person's or public interest to do so – for instance if their life or health is in serious danger. Police forces may therefore exchange information about those likely to commit serious offences, and energy utilities can alert the authorities if power or gas is about to be disconnected – unless the householder has explicitly forbidden such a disclosure. So, if faced with an apparent conflict, just apply common sense, and if necessary consult the Information Commissioner's office. I have always found them to be both helpful and sensible.

GENERAL ELECTIONS

Those UK civil servants who work closely with ministers must maintain strict political impartiality, not least in the weeks before a major election. This section summarises the rules that they must follow.

The term 'purdah' is often used, unofficially, to describe the period immediately after the dissolution of Parliament before an election or referendum, when there are additional restrictions on the activity of civil servants. More literally, it is also called the 'pre-election period'. The term comes from the Urdu and Persian words for veil or curtain, also used to describe the practice of screening women from men or strangers.

Its English usage accordingly suggests Whitehall drawing a veil over itself and cutting itself off as far as possible.

Civil servants may continue to provide ministers with facts that might be used in political speeches etc., and are allowed to check ministers' political speeches for factual accuracy. They are also allowed to comment on the analysis, costings and proposals contained in documents produced by political organisations, including the opposition, but must not draft ministers' responses to such documents.

Unless it runs for the full extent of a fixed term, Parliament is usually dissolved two or three days after the Prime Minister announces the date of the election. If the opposition agrees, this allows the completion of important legislation, such as Finance Bills.

MPs cease to be MPs when Parliament is dissolved. Strictly speaking, therefore, all candidates are thereafter on an equal footing. But it is regarded as courteous for ministers themselves to reply to letters written by MPs before the dissolution, or by former MPs after the dissolution. Private secretary replies are normally sent to candidates (government or opposition) who were not members before the dissolution.

Ministers retain their appointments until the Prime Minister is ready to begin to appoint the next government.

During the pre-election period, the government retains its responsibility to govern and ministers remain in charge of their departments. Essential business must be carried on, but it is customary for ministers to observe discretion as to initiating any new action of a continuing or long-term nature.

Ministers usually try to avoid official engagements because they want to devote the time to campaigning. But they are free to undertake engagements they regard as important, although they should seek to avoid giving the impression that they are using such occasions for party political purposes. Similarly, attendance at some international meetings remains necessary. However, before undertaking to fulfil international commitments, ministers should consider whether the subject matter is such that they can speak with the authority proper to a representative of Her Majesty's Government.

So far as the handling of correspondence is concerned, the general rule is that citizens' individual interests should not be prejudiced by the calling of an election. It follows that letters relating to their interests should be replied to, whether by ministers or by officials on their behalf. But remember that correspondence may become public and might be used for political purposes. Replies to letters should therefore be as straightforward as possible, and should avoid controversy. Letters to election candidates should not distinguish between candidates of different parties, so you should not draft a rather more warm or helpful letter to a candidate who happens to represent your minister's political party.

All public appointments which might be regarded as politically sensitive should be frozen until after the election and, although routine information activities (i.e. the provision of factual information) continue during the election campaign, other information activities generally cease entirely.

This chapter has contained quite a long list of constraints

on civil service (and ministerial) behaviour but it is important not to be daunted by them. I would argue that your most important professional skill is to achieve change whilst behaving properly and responsibly, and that such success brings great personal satisfaction.

Chapter 6

Leadership and Management

W E HAVE ALL attended, or will attend, innu-
merable training programmes, lectures, away
days and the rest aimed at improving the way
we run our organisations. It took me a long
time to realise that the better trainers all said very much the same
things, albeit in different ways and using different words. And
most of the more valuable lessons applied equally to the private,
public and third sectors. Indeed, I have been involved in a number of programmes attended by managers from all three sectors,
and (after initial mutual suspicion) it has always been the case
that they quickly learn that they face very similar problems.

This chapter accordingly summarises the key lessons

imparted by the best leadership and management trainers. Reading these notes will not exempt you from attending such training, but will hopefully help you make sense of it. They will also help you identify the rubbish advice that is offered by the less effective trainers (and your less effective senior managers).

But please bear in mind that these notes do not, and cannot, reflect the unrelenting pace at which modern managers are expected to work. Good managers are supposed to be reflective, organised, rational and plan-oriented. Real managers' work is characterised by brevity, variety and discontinuity. A study of CEOs found that half of managers' activities lasted less than nine minutes. A study of British middle and top managers found that they worked uninterrupted for more than thirty minutes only about once every two days.

Similarly, good managers are trained to empower and delegate. They are told to be like good conductors: they orchestrate everything in advance and then monitor the results. In practice, of course, managers have a number of regular duties that only they can perform. It is a natural part of a manager's job to meet important customers and/or stakeholders, attend retirement parties, meet government officials (or vice versa) and so on.

So although the following advice is sound, it cannot help you find the right mixture of leadership, planning, empowerment, change management and so on that will fit your particular circumstances. But it will certainly help reduce the number of mistakes that you make.

Speaking of which, management is a bit like driving. It's all about taking decisions, often every few seconds – how to react, what tone to adopt, when to change the subject. However hard we try, some of our judgements will be wrong, but hopefully inconsequentially so. Good managers, like good drivers, simply make fewer faulty decisions than others. And firm but fair managers can apologise and move on, for their colleagues recognise their worth and forgive the occasional blemish. Unpopular, unfair managers find that their mistakes are leapt upon as evidence of their inadequacy.

One final point before turning to the detail: just as the manufacturing sector, the retail sector, the tourism sector etc. all face different challenges, so civil service leaders and managers face particular challenges as a result of the political ambitions of their political masters and their opponents. These lead to difficulties when it comes to innovating, and managing big programmes. I comment on these as necessary.

LEADERSHIP

Leadership is about who you are. Management is about what you do. Sir Michael Bichard, a former Permanent Secretary, draws a clear distinction between managers and leaders: 'Managers who control their organisations effectively may enable them to survive. But it is the leaders who create a sense of purpose and direction and who analyse, anticipate and inspire.'

Strong leadership is therefore essential if your team is to be innovative, efficient and successful. And yet one of the minor mysteries of the modern world is why there are so few effective leaders – in both the public and the private sectors – when there is so much advice available in so many different books and courses. Indeed, they all say pretty much the same sort of thing, which is that leaders are different from their followers. They tell their people that they are different and they behave as if they are different. They can answer the following questions from anyone at any time:

- Where are we going?

- Why are we going there?

- How will we get there?

Leaders always have a good number if not all of the following attributes. They:

- have a remorseless iron determination to make things happen;

- have an unshakeable inner conviction;

- lead decisively and confidently;

- constantly promote the same message;

- are different;

- have at least one weakness;

- provide a role model and set an example;

- keep things simple;

- are a little theatrical;

- are authoritative and respected;

- are committed to their team;

- accept blame;

- are honest;

- are physically strong; and

- take risks.

Simple, eh? And of course many civil servants have a good number of the above attributes. But my own observation, for what it is worth, is that too few senior civil servants are sufficiently remorseless, committed, and honest. Let me explain what I mean.

Remorselessness

The first and most important characteristic of a leader is remorselessness, which takes two forms.

First, leaders feel no remorse when they make mistakes, or when some innovation fails to work. They recognise that they are dealing with humans, not machines, and human behaviour is highly unpredictable. Remorse and guilt are understandable, but quite unnecessary, even if something does not work in the way you expected.

Second, leaders are remorseless (in the sense of relentless) because they know that every improvement will take two or three times as long as they expect it to. But they don't let this stop them. Instead, they keep plugging away and eventually they and their teams achieve levels of performance that others can only dream of.

Commitment

Different situations call for different styles of leadership. Sometimes decisions need to be made very quickly and obeyed without question. But leaders nowadays almost always need the consent of those that they lead. Management consultants Kouzes and Posner describe leadership as 'a reciprocal relationship between those who choose to lead and those who decide to follow'. Modern leaders therefore need to be a cross between an old-fashioned captain of a ship and someone who is running for office. It follows that newly appointed leaders should go out of their way to get themselves elected – i.e. respected by their teams – in the first few days after their appointment. This simple fact does not seem to be understood by many colleagues.

Good leaders care for their staff and others. If you are to be elected leader then you must commit to the team, with all its strengths and weaknesses. This is particularly important in the civil service if only because you are unlikely to be around long enough to replace them. And the civil service is anyway so large that, by definition, it has to employ a cross-section of the population. Of course you do not need to put up with mediocrity or laziness. But you cannot insist on surrounding yourself with energetic geniuses. Your task is to get the best out of those who work for you, without forever wishing yourself somewhere else.

How do you show your commitment? You should:

- be very visible, in particular by walking about;

- set a good example, including by complying with rules and standards that have been set for your team;

- champion the team, e.g. by defending them against unfair criticism; but also

- respond to fair criticism, whether of you or your team, in particular by putting matters right and by ensuring that the problem does not recur.

This all seems very obvious, but a middle manager friend of mine told me that three weeks passed before his newly appointed senior civil servant (deputy director) boss got round to meeting him, and he had yet to meet his director after six months in the job. So some colleagues still have something to learn about visibility, commitment and leadership.

Honesty

According to Lucy Kellaway, writing in the *Financial Times*, a good leader knows exactly when to be straight, when to be economical with the truth, when to lay it on with a trowel, and when to dissemble. This is absolutely right, but most of us spend too much time dissembling and too little time being honest with our staff. In particular, we have to be honest in making it clear to staff that they are employed for no other reason than to help the leader achieve his or her objectives. However much they like working together, the team must be directed to achieving a common goal. Everyone is then much better focused and motivated. Those who skirt round this fundamental truth simply waste time and create confused expectations.

Effective leaders also give clear and honest feedback to their staff – not all the time, but frequently enough to encourage good, or deter bad, behaviour. Any sustained failure to give honest feedback to colleagues – and of course we have all failed to some extent, and regretted it – can only end in disappointment, confusion and demoralisation. Honest appraisal is also a necessary companion to empowerment. Once the manager has defined the job that is to be done, he or she should aim to keep out of the way and let his or her staff do what is expected

of them. But there must be regular informal and formal appraisal to ensure that the work stays on track.

But...

The problem with my pen picture of an effective leader
is that it equally well describes Winston Churchill and Adolf
Hitler, Nelson Mandela and Stalin. So we need to distinguish
good leaders from strong leaders. What marks them out? It
is clearly the culture that they encourage, and the boundaries
that they set.

The best leaders carry out a difficult balancing act. On the
one hand they need to be obsessive about setting the correct
boundaries and establishing the right culture. On the other
hand, they need to empower and support. Those who get it
right can usually then stand back and watch their team achieve
surprising results. Further detail follows...

Setting Boundaries

It is vitally important that leaders should establish the ethical, financial, legal and other boundaries within which their
colleagues should work. Problems (and sometimes severe
problems) arise when these are not explicit or, even worse,
when senior managers appear themselves not to respect those
boundaries. It is particularly important that civil servants
should operate within the ethical, financial and legal boundaries laid down by Parliament and it is odd, to say the least,
that it is difficult to find a written statement of these. I hope that
other parts of this book go some way to defining the boundaries

of which I am aware. It follows that I require everyone who works with me to respect these boundaries and to require all their staff to do the same.

Many boundaries are cultural, rather than ethical, in the sense that leaders are responsible for establishing the parameters within which staff deal with each other, with customers, with work pressures and so on. There is more on this below, but it is worth noting that some staff will constantly test your boundaries and force your intervention when the boundaries are likely to be breached. They will then accuse you of micromanagement. Other staff will respect your boundaries and get on with their jobs with very little intervention from you. But as a result, they may worry that you are not interested in them or their work area. It is therefore important that you explain your approach, and reassure those who think you have taken empowerment just a little too far.

Establishing the Culture

Leaders set the tone of the organisation – even in small but important ways. For instance, I hope that any visitor to my office will find that we are open, informal and hospitable. We feel that it makes a real difference if we are friendly and polite to each other, and offer refreshments and other courtesies to visitors. We in particular welcome the opportunity to talk about our work, and our approach to our work, and welcome visits from colleagues from embassies, from industrialists, from students and from teachers.

I also expect everyone to recognise their responsibility for the safety, health and well-being of themselves and all their colleagues. We take the alarm bells seriously, even if we suspect that they are a false alarm. We take seriously all reports of sexual harassment, racial or sexual discrimination, or bullying. We give unquestioning support to colleagues who express concern about safety, harassment or discrimination. Above all, we do not ask colleagues to work so hard that they become stressed or over-tired. This is not only unethical, but it leads to mistakes and misjudgements – which in turn create more pressure.

Next, I encourage everyone to be customer-focused, where our customers are defined as the immediate beneficiaries of particular pieces of work. If you are preparing a briefing, your customer is the person who will use it. If you are organising a meeting, your customers will be those who attend the meeting. Our customers should be the sole and decisive judge of the quality of our work. The test is not whether we think that our work meets the requirements of the customer, but whether the customer is satisfied.

This implies measurement. You cannot tell whether your customer is satisfied unless you have asked him or her in a structured way. It should become second nature that your plans and your day-to-day work are driven by the expressed needs of your customers.

Measurement in turn drives continuous improvement. You and your team should constantly be looking out for ways – usually quite small in themselves – in which you could improve the satisfaction of the customer, or do the job more efficiently or effectively. The cumulative effort of many small improvements can be very noticeable indeed. Conversely, a cumulative failure to improve will eventually and inevitably lead to your customers feeling dissatisfied with the service that you are providing. It follows that imitation is a virtue. If you hear of a good idea, or see something working well, you should not hesitate to copy it so as to improve the service that you are providing to your customers. And if you run out of ideas for improvements, you should benchmark your team against another team or organisation. You will probably be surprised at what you find.

Continuous improvement in turn requires a no-fault culture. We assume that everyone is trying to do a good job, within the limits of their skills, training and experience. Management gurus often say that 'customers' complaints are jewels to be treasured'. This is a bit over the top for most of us, but it is certainly true that complaints should never be ignored, and a single complaint often represents the tip of an iceberg of unvoiced dissatisfaction. Quality-conscious organisations are therefore usually obsessive about investigating and resolving customer complaints, whether from internal or external customers. And complaints should never be used as a stick with which to beat your staff or other colleagues. If mistakes are made, or if quality standards are not met, then the person involved should be given clearer instructions or better training, or attention must be given to the process that they were carrying out, or to whether they are in an appropriate job. (This judgement should not be arrived at lightly, but neither should it be ducked. If necessary, the person must be moved to a job that they can do.)

Empowerment

Empowerment is often confused with delegation. Delegation often means no more than that the delegate is simply told what to do and how to do it. Empowerment is better because it allows the colleague to choose how best to achieve his or her objectives and targets. Leaders don't delegate. They empower.

But note that empowerment is not a close relation of anarchy. People work to clearly specified objectives and targets, which they may not vary without consulting their boss and/or customer. Also, as noted above, they must work within other constraints laid down by the manager, including appropriate professional standards, quality standards, financial constraints and standard procedures. You should help them gain experience by empowering them, monitoring their performance and acting to relax the constraints as soon as you can.

In particular, submissions, draft letters etc. should be prepared by the person, however junior, best equipped to prepare a first draft. If the issue is not novel or contentious, and the person is appropriately experienced and trained, then there should be no need for the work to be countersigned by anyone else. Two heads are however better than one if an issue is novel or contentious. A senior colleague who countersigns work in these circumstances should concentrate on the substance of the work, and the way it will appear to ministers or the recipients of letters etc. They should pay relatively little attention to the detail, style or grammar of the work.

Work should also be countersigned if the action officer is being trained, or gaining experience. It is helpful in these circumstances if the countersigning officer pays attention both to the substance of the work and to the detail, style and grammar. The objective of this intervention should, however, be to train the colleague so that countersignature is in due course not necessary.

MANAGEMENT

Leadership and management are inseparable – the two sides of the same coin – and yet quite different. Management is the process of getting the most out of the resources at your disposal, and in particular getting the most out of your team.

Most processes involve the following:

1. Establish the identity of your customer: the person (a minister?) that you are trying to please – not necessarily (or usually) the person who is managing you.

2. Establish (with your customer) your objectives. How will the customer know whether you have done what he or she wanted?

3. Create and motivate an appropriate team, and identify what other resources you will need.

4. Choose an appropriate strategy – best thought of as the route that will most efficiently get you to your objective – and then develop a more detailed plan, at least for the first few stages.

5. Measure progress towards the objective, using milestones as necessary.

6. Revise the strategy and detailed plan as and when necessary.

Setting Objectives

Civil servants have traditionally drafted their own objectives or job plan. This approach was unfortunately enshrined in official guidance when objective-setting was first introduced in 1986. Why 'unfortunately'? It is surely axiomatic that managers should take responsibility for defining what jobs they want done, what sort of person they want to do them and what standard of performance is expected. This should be clearly set out in a document which draws as necessary on the department's and directorate's written objectives, and should in the first instance be drafted by the manager, not the managed. After all, who else but the manager can in the first instance say why a particular individual is employed within their team?

And too many civil servants default to job descriptions that are all about what people do ('I give policy advice...', 'I manage...') rather than what they are trying to achieve. The usual response is that things like the health of an industry, or of the population, are dependent upon so many variables that it is positively unfair to credit any one civil servant with their improvement. There is of course some truth in this but it is also true that a great deal of effort will be wasted unless it is directed towards an identifiable (even if distant) objective. Also, the adoption of challenging and worthwhile objectives leads quickly to innovation, team-work and other good practices.

Objectives should be 'SMART', i.e. specific, measurable, agreed, realistic and time-dependent. And they should be kept simple and relevant to the person who owns them. For instance, few of us can cope with more than the three tiers of aims, objectives and targets. And whilst an objective of the Permanent Secretary of the Home Office might be to cut crime, or keep it to a certain figure, this would become part of the vision of more junior officials who might be responsible for the police pension scheme. The important thing is that those in charge of the pension scheme should know that it needs to be so designed that it will attract and retain high-calibre police officers (and that is their objective), in order that they might cut crime.

And if anyone has difficulty in accepting worthwhile objectives, as distinct from day-to-day targets and activities, it is helpful to ask them what would change, or how they and their team would be missed, if they did not exist. Alternatively, the line manager should complete the sentence beginning 'You will be a success if you...' I have yet to meet anyone who has, when challenged in this way, failed to justify their employment in terms of meaningful objectives.

But note that it is genuinely difficult for some senior officials to be explicit about their and hence their ministers' objectives, for ministers will often *either* refuse to be specific (for fear of being seen to fail) *or* announce some dramatic objective which, within days, appears imprecise or unattainable.

And take care! Objectives are powerful things, especially when linked (as they should be) to appraisal. Get them wrong and your whole organisation will go off in the wrong direction. Take particular care if you are tempted to define your objectives in monetary terms. This approach can sometimes be very effective. Equally, it can turn you all into novice accountants, quite oblivious to your wider or longer-term responsibilities. See also the advice on measurement in the section on planning, below.

Although the job plan should emphasise the importance of achieving worthwhile objectives, rather than the ability to demonstrate a range of grade-related skills or behaviour, it should also make it clear what levels of skill, effort and achievement represent satisfactory performance. This will help those who wish to show that their performance has been much better than satisfactory. It can also be useful to deploy the concept of 'breakthrough performance' when trying to explain the difference between what is in the civil service generally known as 'Box 2' rather than 'Box 3' (i.e. satisfactory) performance.

Although I always write the first draft of the person's objectives, the document obviously has to be shown in draft to the person being managed. In particular, I have often found it helpful to ask colleagues to say, in effect, what they offer to do by way of satisfactory performance. This can help dispel unreal expectations that satisfactory performance somehow deserves an exceptional report. Indeed, I take the firm view that Box 2 breakthrough performance cannot be recognised in the absence of a clear agreement between manager and managed which specifies the level of performance that has been exceeded.

Planning and Measurement

Having set your objectives, you must now plan how you will get there.

Planning is of course an unnatural process. It is, after all, much more fun to do something. And the other nice thing about not planning is that failure comes as a complete surprise rather than being preceded by a period of worry and depression. But experienced managers know that planning is (a) relatively simple (which is perhaps another reason why it does not appeal to many civil servants) and (b) an indispensable precursor to success. The main thing, therefore, is to do it! But when you do it, these are the key points that need to be borne in mind:

- Keep it simple;

- Focus on results, i.e. what is to be achieved;

- Ensure individual responsibility for all members of the team,

LEADERSHIP AND MANAGEMENT 205
project into constituent parts which are the responsibility of
named individuals;
- Communicate, and in particular clearly communicate both
objectives and progress both within and outside the team;

- Monitor progress both carefully and frequently.

Much of the above implies measurement. This lies at the heart
of effective management, whether of the policy process or of
anything else. We all know – though we often forget – that
'you cannot manage what you do not measure'. Another version of this saying is: 'If you measure it, you change it' – which
leads to the conclusion that you should 'make the important
measurable, not the measurable important'. This really is
the key to success in all your endeavours, and time spent on
unmeasured activity is the most likely time to be wasted.

The following sections focus on particular management
skills.

RECRUITMENT

To begin at the beginning, management is clearly much easier if you can recruit the right people and then guide them
successfully. But it is very hard to get it right, partly because
we are often reluctant to spell out exactly what attributes we

don't want, as well as what we do want. There is, for instance, plenty of room for shy, retiring, academic individuals in some parts of the civil service, but many Whitehall and other jobs require staff to be friendly, self-starting, clear communicators and so on. These attributes need to be spelt out and appraised, or else you will end up appointing an unemployable genius – great at completing crosswords but quite incapable of making decisions or managing fellow humans with all their faults and frailties.

It must be recognised, too, that recruitment, whether from inside or outside the civil service, is particularly risky because you don't have a lot of time to get to know the candidate before appointment. You must therefore be ready to accept that some appointments will not work, through no fault on the part of you or the appointee. But here are some thoughts that might help you cut the error rate.

Take care to ensure that the job description and person specification are comprehensive. If you need the appointee to be friendly, approachable and flexible, then this needs to be spelt out in advance. Equally, if the job can be filled by a shy, backroom sort of person, then other attributes will need to be stressed. You may find Nancy Holloway's advice at Annex C helpful in framing both the person specification and subsequent lines of questioning.

Do not put too much weight on performance in the traditional 45-minute interview. Some candidates think much more quickly than others, and/or are more able to express their thoughts orally. These may be important attributes – but in many cases you will be better off appointing a deeper thinker, or someone who takes time to order their thoughts in a way that allows them to communicate more clearly – especially in writing.

It is much better, therefore, to arrange for shortlisted candidates to have two discussions (not 'interviews') with two different halves of a four-person recruitment panel. This facilitates a much deeper investigation of the candidates' interests, character, strengths and weaknesses. This may seem time-consuming, but it is a lot less time-consuming than dealing with the aftermath of a less than optimal appointment.

Do encourage genuine diversity. Your approach should *not* be 'Come in and we'll show you how to be like us.' It should be 'Come in … and now we are a new organisation.' Even today, women seeking promotion often feel the need to be 'the right sort of chap' in both background and behaviour. This needs to stop.

Similarly, do not demand sophisticated drafting skills from everyone. There is a marked waste of talent in many departments because good managers, good networkers – especially with those in industry – good 'deliverers', and many professionals are deemed unsuited to working closely with ministers.

It is also much better to rank candidates in advance of final discussion/interview drawing on a careful (and sceptical/evidence-based) review of their achievements in previous jobs. The discussions can then be used to test the accuracy of the ranking rather than as an event on which the whole process hinges.

Take care not to be fooled by embellished and exaggerated CVs, but do take oral references in advance of discussion/interview. Having learned from bitter experience, I would not appoint to a middle-ranking or senior position without taking a quite deep prior reference. Some candidates cannot supply these for good reasons, but others cannot provide them because they have been dismissed for incompetence or worse. It is seldom worth taking the risk.

Equally, do take a moment to think about the motivation of the referee. Some managers are trying to get rid of poor-quality staff, and hope you will end up holding this particular damaged parcel. And some will bad-mouth staff who do not fit their particular mould, although you might rather welcome a recruit who is a little out of the ordinary.

Do not downplay the difficult aspects of the job for which you are recruiting. Many public-facing positions, for instance, and jobs in ministers' offices, are very stressful, as are jobs (such as some regulatory jobs) whose outputs are subject to intense scrutiny, including by the courts. The need for these positions to be filled by robust personalities must be spelt out to all candidates as it is no kindness to them (or you) if they are appointed to a job in which they cannot succeed.

There is no need to ask all the candidates the same questions. Although the job specification is the same for all candidates, their experience and apparent strengths will vary, so your questions need to vary if you are to accurately assess their suitability for the job.

And don't forget the need for high-quality induction to

follow any recruitment process. This is too often neglected, especially in the case of senior appointments; this is one of the reasons why I wrote this book.

It is particularly important that new entrants to the profession are introduced to the Civil Service Code, and come to understand its importance and implications. There should be no question of local mission statements or departmental core values overriding the provisions of the code.

APPRAISAL

The formal appraisal system may be a necessary evil, although I note that its value is these days frequently questioned by both academics and management consultants. Informal appraisal is certainly much more effective, perhaps along the lines summarised in the book *The One-Minute Manager*. This suggests that managers should give immediate feedback whenever they see good or bad work. Unfortunately, too many managers give immediate feedback that is either always positive (and therefore dishonest) or always negative (which is debilitating). Colleagues quickly learn to appreciate the honesty of the manager who gives both sorts of feedback.

Formal appraisal is delivered within a structured system over which individual managers have only limited control. But it is worth making four important points.

First, the formal annual appraisal is essentially one-way communication. The process might begin with self-appraisal (although I have my doubts about the effectiveness of this approach) but it is essentially an opportunity for the appraiser to be honest about how the other person has appeared to them over the preceding period. The person being appraised might well feel that the appraiser is wrong, but that should lead to improved communication and other action in the next reporting period. There should be no question of the appraisal being 'agreed' by the person being appraised, or subject to any form of appeal.

It is sensible, however, to show draft appraisals to the person on whom you are reporting, for you might well have forgotten some achievement, or you might have expressed something in an upsetting way. But the report should nevertheless remain your honest assessment of the other person, in comparison to other civil servants.

Second, appraisals should lead to action, whether by way of improved communication between manager and managed, or changes to objectives and expectations, or further training and development.

Third, keep it simple! No one remembers the detail of an appraisal more than a few hours after reading it. When I ran a small department, we categorised staff as very effective, effective or not effective, and this worked very well, especially if allowance was explicitly made for those who were in the process of gaining experience.

Fourth, it is better if appraisals are supplemented by 'upward feedback' or even '360-degree feedback'. There are several good systems that facilitate these processes but it must be stressed that they need to be carefully managed if they are to do more good than harm. They should certainly not amount to 'upward appraisal'. Managers should want to know what messages their staff believe they are receiving, in particular through the managers' behaviour. But it is not for staff to tell managers whether the messages are appropriate, or whether the manager is regarded as doing a good job. There may be some saints who would respond enthusiastically to criticism from inexperienced staff, but I fear that I and many others are not amongst them – at least until I have worked with my critics for a good long time.

Remember, too, that we all have different mixtures of experiences, strengths and weaknesses. One or two weaknesses may be quite irrelevant in the current job, and should not be used to mark a person down. Equally, it is often the case that a single weakness can be a major problem, and this needs to be spelt out and addressed. Too many senior officials have reached their current positions despite being inexperienced or poor managers, simply because they score well when it comes to analytical ability and the like. It would be much better for all concerned if such weaknesses could be addressed early in such careers, and regarded as an absolute bar to further progress.

BUILDING SUCCESSFUL TEAMS – AND DOES MORALE MATTER?

Much has been written about how to create and build successful teams, but Judy Foster summarised it very well when she stressed that there are five key enabling factors:

1. Coherent policies;

2. Effective professional development;

3. A sense of autonomy: the ability to innovate in response to customers' needs;

4. Sound support structures, including well-run and genuinely participative management meetings;

5. Sufficient mental space to be able to process difficult emotional situations, see clearly and think creatively. This includes supportive supervision provided by more experienced colleagues.

Judy's research showed that mental space is particularly vital – and in short supply in some of the social work teams that she studied. I suspect that much the same can be said of many civil service teams who spend too much time attending inefficient meetings and/or fire-fighting in response to short-term pressures, and taking far too little time to think clearly and creatively.

Morale, by the way, just like happiness, is surprisingly elusive. It is a great mistake to try directly to improve morale. Good morale comes naturally to any well-managed team, and never comes to a team that is poorly led, lacks clear objectives, is poorly trained or lacks good honest communication. So if you lead and manage well, high morale will inevitably follow, however difficult the surrounding circumstances.

Do also bear in mind that morale will inevitably dip during a period of rapid change. The team does not at first realise that it needs to change. (This state is sometimes unkindly referred to as 'unconscious incompetence'.) Once it faces up to its problems then confidence and morale will inevitably decline ('conscious incompetence'). It will then begin to do better, although perhaps rather self-consciously ('conscious competence') and finally morale will rise rapidly once the new way of working has become second nature ('unconscious competence'). It is then the job of the leader to ensure that this state is maintained for as long as possible, through seeking continuous improvement, so that the team does not slip back into unconscious incompetence.

Chapter 7

Innovation and Project Management

INNOVATION

THERE IS PERSISTENT criticism that the civil service too often fails to identify innovative solutions to policy problems. There is some truth in this, for the following reasons:

1. We work for politicians, who in turn work in an adversarial and confrontational environment, under constant media scrutiny.

It is the duty of the opposition to oppose. New ideas are swiftly attacked, improvements are regarded as evidence of past failure, debates about the merits of particular proposals are seized upon as signs of divisions within government, and mistakes are mercilessly exposed and criticised. Ministers do not like to be outshone by exciting, achieving and innovative officials, and do not thank us for exposing them to criticism for some new idea which has not yet been properly thought through. Any potentially controversial idea that cannot be kept entirely secret is therefore best left well alone.

2. We are part of a profession, and cannot afford to alienate colleagues with whom we might have to work very closely for years to come. Also, our professional and financial rewards come mainly via promotion. It is therefore vital that we do not do anything which might upset a senior colleague, and in particular our manager and our Permanent Secretary. We therefore: do not encourage internal challenge; hesitate before saying anything which might be construed as foolish by any senior colleague – most of whom will be older than us; and are reluctant to draw attention to colleagues, or parts of a department, who are performing badly – and yet this is often a necessary precursor to real change.

3. We work within quite distinct government departments, with quite distinct budgets and for ministers who are usually in competition with their colleagues in other departments. We develop a loyalty to the organisation, to our staff, to our budget and to our ministers, which tends to inhibit free thinking.

4. The effort required to complete maybe several rounds of consultation within government can be quite daunting.

5. Our work is dominated by major and apparently unquestionable policies, including those in manifestos. There are therefore significant limits to the extent to which we are permitted to think the unthinkable.

Against the above, let me make four important points.

1. Other organisations find it equally difficult to foster internal challenge and innovation. Indeed, variations on all the above problems, apart perhaps from the first and fourth, can be found in most other large professions and organisations.

2. There is nothing inherent in our two key professional duties (to give independent, balanced advice, and to implement ministers' decisions, even if we have advised against them) that stops us being innovative.

3. There is no suggestion that we should all become innovative or creative all the time. But those of us who are innovative – and when we are innovative – need to operate in a supportive environment.

4. Being innovative is not the same as being entrepreneurial. Whatever they may say, no one, and least of all our ministers, wants us to treat public money as if it were our own, or do deals other than within clearly established boundaries.

So here are a few thoughts that may help you create innovative teams.

The key point is that teams become innovative when they are well led, truly empowered within clear boundaries, and measured by results. In addition, you have to encourage a little rebellion and a questioning culture. Allow people, if they wish, to squirrel away a little time to work on pet projects. Expose problems – otherwise they will not get solved – and reward innovation through pay and promotion as well as in less tangible ways. Do not create a team that is excessively harmonious, for this stifles innovation.

Next, I want to stress the value of planning. The first thing to do, once you have a bright idea, is to decide the extent of the likely opposition and plan a strategy for overcoming it. Don't be reassured by ministers' and senior colleagues' well-meant protestations that they adore innovative and risk-taking officials. In practice, innovation is fine if there is relatively little political interest in the activity. It is also easier to innovate if you are working closely with customers, and responding to clear customer pressure. That is why colleagues in many agencies and local offices find it relatively easy to innovate, if their head offices do not hold them back. In contrast, just imagine the obstacles that would face the prison service in the unlikely event that they found a way of halving the recidivism rate, but at the cost of doubling the number of escapes. They would have to plan their innovation strategy very carefully, enlisting strong ministerial support, gaining buy-in within the wider service (which would take time), and – above all

– becoming very innovative in managing their relationship with the media.

THE FEAR OF RISK

Because ministers are publicly accountable, they are understandably reluctant to make mistakes that might expose them to criticism, even if only with the benefit of hindsight. Their officials should therefore be aware of the risks associated with various courses of action. But you will never achieve anything if your principal career objective is never to make a mistake. You should therefore aim to be risk-conscious rather than risk-averse. It is helpful to think in terms of a spectrum of risk.

There will be high risk if the suggested action will commit a great deal of money or other resource; if the repercussions from the action are unpredictable; if there is a history of serious error in this area; if the decision is of significant political or media interest; if there will be many losers and/or if there will be a small number of heavy losers. If these features are present then do not rush the decision. You should consult and plan very carefully, and if possible test the water by piloting any new scheme or activity, so as to test its practicality in the real world. In other words: 'Don't bet the business.'

There is low risk if an error would have little cost, is unlikely, could easily be corrected and/or is of little political or media interest. In this case, do not delay and keep consultation to the absolute minimum. Get on with it! Far too many civil servants agonise at length over minor decisions and rush the major ones. They obey the well-known law that the time devoted to the decision is in inverse proportion to its importance. Feel free to break this particular law!

But there are many intermediate cases where decisions carry medium risk. In these cases you should ask 'Why not?' rather than 'Why?'. Try out the idea on one or two interested observers, without exhaustively arguing the pros and cons. If there is no strong opposition, then, again, get on with it without further consultation. Otherwise, think through the issue again – and especially those aspects that have concerned those you have consulted.

There is no need to worry all the time about possible Public Accounts Committee or media criticism of minor decisions. Such criticism is generally concentrated on major decisions where the risks were clearly high, and the spending or action clearly inappropriate. Indeed, Sir John Bourn, head of the National Audit Office, said: 'The problem is not that the Whitehall culture is risk-averse .... Rather, it is risk-ignorant. It takes the most fantastic risks without knowing it is doing so.' Therefore, as long as you are conscious of the scale of the risk associated with your decision, and prepared to justify your decision on that basis, whilst recognising that others might well have decided differently, you will not receive serious criticism. All this was neatly summarised by Sir David Omand who, when Permanent Secretary at the Home Office, told his colleagues: 'If you are not making mistakes, you are not trying hard enough.'

OTHER DEPARTMENTS

The strongest opposition to any innovative policy will inevitably come from other departments, fuelled by *departmentalitis*. Gerald Kaufman MP first drew attention to this debilitating ministerial disease in his excellent book *How to Be a Minister*, first published in 1980:

> If you contract departmentalitis you will ruthlessly pursue your own department's interests even if another department has a better case: quite simply, your department must win ... you will forget that you are part of a government, that the fortunes of the government are more important than the fortunes of your own department.

But the disease is also endemic amongst officials. We kid ourselves that we run a finely tuned machine, co-ordinating and consulting effectively with colleagues elsewhere in government. The truth is that large groups – and indeed whole departments – all too often compete with one another with the result that progress is too slow and we make too many mistakes. As a result, the whole system can begin to break down, and can sometimes break down completely.

The correct treatment for this disease is to refuse to play our cards close to our chest, and refuse to seek power by failing to share information. Remember in particular that ministers may not order us not to consult or give relevant information to colleagues who have a right to be consulted or to know what is going on. It is of course sometimes sensible to work up a proposal before showing it to colleagues. But you may not collude in a 'bounce' and if you feel that colleagues in another department would expect to be told about a proposal, then you must tell them. Officials in different departments should also try very hard to resolve differences without involving ministers. It is stupid and inefficient to conduct an argument between officials through ministerial correspondence. This should be reserved for genuine debate between ministers.

Of course it is no bad thing to become emotionally committed to achieving your, or your minister's, objectives, as long as you remain politically impartial, well-balanced and professional. But you should not set out to browbeat colleagues by arguing as if your preference is self-evidently optimal. Such certainty can sometimes impress colleagues, and can sometimes sway decisions. But it is unprofessional and leads to decisions that are not soundly based. If your minister's view does not seem to stand up to critical onslaught, you need to go back and discuss the problem. You should not simply try to bulldoze his or her view through.

And we should not hesitate to seek help from colleagues, even at the risk of appearing a little silly. Colleagues collectively have a wealth of knowledge and experience. Even if the problem is quite novel, they will have ideas about how you might tackle it. Indeed, most problems melt away if you simply seek help from colleagues. Almost everyone is more than willing to help, if they are approached in the right way. Indeed, it is often a very good idea to brainstorm an issue or to think aloud. But you should flag up very clearly that this is what you are doing, or else colleagues will think that you are delivering a considered view, and will not be impressed by your more hare-brained ideas!

You may occasionally come across someone – perhaps in a central department or in an influential position elsewhere in your department – who will seem to give you a direct order that you are not happy to accept. Remember that they cannot do so. No official other than in your management chain can give you an order, even if they are in No. 10, in the Cabinet Office, or even in your solicitor's office. They can draw your attention to their minister's views, or to established policy, or to the law, and you will usually wish to take careful note. But in the last resort you must be guided by your own professional opinion. If you were to follow their advice, and they were to turn out to have been wrong, you could not subsequently blame them. If they continue to press their case, and you remain unpersuaded, you should consult ministers or (in the case of legal advice) your department's senior legal adviser.

Finally, a word about dealing with the Treasury and the Foreign and Commonwealth Office (FCO). Officials from these two departments tend to wield more power than others. This derives from the status of their ministers and, in the case of the Treasury, from the fact that they act as HMG's banker. But the nature of their work means that some of them have little first-hand experience of their subject, or of achieving change. They are therefore required to question your policies without being expected to know the underlying facts. As a result, a small minority of Treasury and FCO colleagues give the impression that they believe that other departments are not clever enough, are not critical enough and do not work hard enough. In practice it is not too difficult to prove them wrong, as long as you are indeed fully on top of your policy issues and the associated facts. If they can ask a relevant question that flummoxes you, you have only yourself to blame. The vast majority of Treasury and FCO staff are in fact very professional, experienced in their fields and invaluable colleagues. You should therefore treat them as equals, and expect them to treat you likewise.

PROGRAMME AND PROJECT MANAGEMENT

'The British government spends an unfathomable £670 billion every year – and often does so in ways that are wasteful and misguided.' So begins the cover blurb for *Conundrum: Why Every Government Gets Things Wrong* by Richard Bacon MP and Christopher Hope. The book contains a depressing and all-too-familiar catalogue of badly designed and implemented major programmes, but its central thesis is that delivery is too often the poor relation to policy for both ministers and civil servants. The following advice does not aim to remedy all the faults identified by Messrs Bacon and Hope, but – if you were to follow it – it would certainly improve matters.

To begin at the beginning: the words 'programme' and 'project' are, in most cases, interchangeable. The key thing is that they conceptually follow on from a policy decision – a decision that will hopefully have taken account of the practical, financial and other factors that will constrain the delivery of that policy. (See the earlier chapter in this book for advice on policy design.) In theory, a programme is large-scale, and often consists of a number of projects. But a project can be pretty big too, and can certainly appear very challenging to those in charge of it. Programmes and projects should therefore be managed in pretty much the same way, using the approach outlined below.

Significant projects should of course be led by people with proper project management training and experience, and the civil service has recruited a good number of these in recent years. Mainstream officials are more likely to be heavily involved in the policy development and project definition phase of major projects and then acting as the principal customer of a specialist project/programme manager. But almost any civil servant could find him/herself responsible for a smaller project. In either case the following advice is very relevant.

It is first worth noting that the initiation of a major government project can be a very sudden affair. Presidents and Prime Ministers feel under great pressure to announce dramatic goals. Some of these work out OK, such as Kennedy's 1961 belief that 'this nation should commit itself to achieving the goal, before this decade is out, of landing a man on the moon and returning him safely to the Earth'. Neil Armstrong stepped onto the Sea of Tranquillity in 1969. Some don't turn out quite so well. I'll leave you to think of your own UK examples.

And many lesser mortals can fall into the trap of what the World Bank tactfully calls 'appraisal optimism' – the presentation of best-case scenarios including underestimated costs and timescales, and overestimated benefits, in order to get projects started. A less tactful phrase is 'conspiracy of optimism'. There are plenty of examples, including London's Barbican Centre (estimated cost £8 million, actual cost £187 million), the Humber Bridge (£28 million / £151 million), the British Library (£74 million / £511 million) and the Jubilee Line extension (£2.1 billion / £3.5 billion). These examples perhaps support the seductive proposition that nothing would ever get built without a little massaging of the facts and figures, but such behaviour inevitably leads to later criticism of the officials responsible for the project, rather than the politicians who pressed for it to proceed.

The National Audit Office has listed the following perennial problems:

- Civil servants may be reluctant to highlight unrealistic timescales or the need for further pilots and planning, as they want to be seen as 'can do'.

- This can generate pressure to hurry the implementation of reforms and projects.

- However, sustainable changes to public services need a strategic perspective, careful planning and sound implementation.

- If a department can only move at a slow pace, it can be detrimental to value for money to pretend otherwise.

- A department may also only be able to take on so much change at once.

- There is no deliberate resistance to ministers' demands. Instead, there is unacknowledged reality.

And here is the NAO's summary of what happens when officials ignore inconvenient facts – as they do:

- There is pressure to present the unlikely upside as the most likely result.

- Major projects under-deliver on benefits and overshoot on time and cost.

- There is optimism-bias.

- Changing requirements lead to delays and increases in costs, for example in major defence projects. (The first rule of procurement is: 'Once you have decided what you want, don't fiddle around with it.')

It follows, therefore, that you should do your best to persuade an enthusiastic minister that more haste equals less speed, even though they may feel that you are dragging your feet and/or seeing unnecessary obstacles. They may, however, recognise the thought that there is a natural rhythm to a good project – nice and slow and cautious at the beginning, so that rapid pre-planned progress can be made at the end. It is a trite but accurate observation that a new building will soon be finished after its foundations have been laid. Ministers will still need to make those big bold announcements, if only to forestall the announcement of a similar ambition by a rival. But such announcements should explicitly allow you time to research and plan the project in some detail.

There is another trap, in that some projects look to be obviously sensible when a bit of research would have shown the opposite. The classic example is the 1970 'Scared Straight!' project in the United States, where juvenile delinquents were exposed to inmates in local prisons with a view to persuading the kids to turn away from a life of crime. Nearly forty years on, these projects are still being started, although the evidence strongly suggests that they increase criminality, not reduce it.

Here, then, is a sensible checklist for each stage of a large project, including nine key questions that must be answered before there is full commitment to the desired objective.

Initiation and Planning

Before you do anything else, sit down and think hard about the following issues:

- What is the result you want to achieve?

- What are the causal factors that influence that result?

- What policy interventions will make a difference?

- What is the evidence?

- Who do you rely on to deliver?

You should also think hard, up front, about the following three critical factors for successful delivery.

Critical Success Factor 1: The right scope. Any investment of time or money must be linked to clear outcomes that support strategic objectives. And goals must be realistic and based on knowledge of what is achievable.

Critical Success Factor 2: Adequate skills and resources, matched to the demands of the programme/project.

Critical Success Factor 3: Good processes for delivery based on approaches that are likely to work.

Planning for Delivery

Once you have thought long and hard about the above issues, you must make sure that ministers and other key stakeholders agree with your conclusions before you settle down to detailed planning. The following are the nine main questions you will need to answer. You should therefore prepare and circulate, including to ministers, a detailed plan which answers each of these questions.

1. What is the scope? What is to be delivered – and when?

2. What resources and capabilities (people, physical resources and funding) will you need?

3. What are the potential sources of such capabilities?

4. Who will carry out the required processes and policies?

5. Who will be accountable for what?

6. Which similar projects have succeeded – and why?

7. What is an acceptable balance of cost, benefit and risk? And how should they be managed?

8. How you will work with other delivery agents and stakeholders to share information and knowledge?

9. How will you monitor and report progress? What performance measures and incentives will you need?

There are more detailed notes on each of these subjects at Annex D.

Finally, remember the very well-known frequent causes of failure:

- Unclear objectives and success criteria;

- Insufficient involvement of key stakeholders;

- Weak risk management;

- Unclear roles and responsibilities;

- Lack of appropriate skills;

- Weak financial control;

- Poor market knowledge;

- Inadequate understanding of IT challenges.

They won't happen on your watch, will they!

MANAGING CHANGE

Whitehall officials spend much of their time initiating or implementing change. Indeed, ministers, the media and the public often demand to see high-profile and rapid change, despite the frequency with which such programmes have been seen to fail – and despite the fact that change is seldom win–win, and the losers may eventually be much more vociferous than the gainers. So how can you reduce the chance of failure? Every change programme has its own characteristics, of course, but you should never forget the five Cs – the five elements of any organisation, none of which can be changed without simultaneously causing change in the others:

- Capacity, i.e. resources, and in particular staff numbers;

- Capability (or competence), i.e. staff skills, training, experience and motivation;

- Communications, including not only communications whilst the change programme is being implemented, but also new ways of communicating once the changes have been implemented;

- Culture, new relationships, attitudes to innovation, reward structures etc.;

- Constitution, i.e. organisational structure, reporting lines etc.

Any significant change process must consider the inter-relationship between these five elements, and what all of them – not just one of them – will look like at the end of the process. For instance, downsizing or de-layering might need to be accompanied by changes in the other elements, including improved training and team-work, employing fewer, more highly quali-fied (and higher-paid) staff, accepting lower service quality, and accepting more frequent errors. A failure to think along these lines will mean that the slimmed-down organisation will per-form markedly less well, and may even return to its former size when it is forced to recruit again to improve its performance.

It follows that it is very difficult to manage change successfully, which is why so many reform and change programmes are unsuccessful. That is why there is so much to be said for opting instead for continuous improvement of existing processes and structures, if ministers and others will be patient enough. Natural staff turnover (often 10 to 20 per cent per annum) permits rapid cost saving, whilst the experience and commitment of existing staff and customers help managers focus on those areas that need, and will benefit from, urgent improvement.

Chapter 8

Personal Effectiveness

THERE IS LOTS of written material, not to mention training programmes etc., aimed at improving our personal effectiveness. But much of it repackages the same advice in different ways. This chapter summarises the key things that I have learned over the years, including from experience in the office. I have divided the subjects as follows:

- Managing Personal Relationships;

- Managing Meetings;

- Managing Negotiations;

- Managing Our Own Time;

- Whose Problem Is It Anyway?

MANAGING PERSONAL RELATIONSHIPS

Here are a few techniques that can be used if you feel that you are not getting on with, or not getting through to, someone who is important to you – a concerned member of the public, perhaps, or your boss, or a minister.

First, pay attention to the need for clear communication. Use simple, unambiguous language, and clearly explain the reasons for your proposals or requirements. Never get angry and always be polite (but not unctuous). Remember that aggressive and demanding people often have fairly thick skins. And obsessive people often feel that something is being hidden from them. Tell both sorts of person that you intend, if they agree, not to beat about the bush. They will always agree, and then you can deal with any problem in blunt terms.

Next, pay attention to your relative status. We all communicate with each other as superiors, as equals or as inferiors and we frequently adopt different approaches to the same person at different times. Problems invariably arise, in work as well as at home, when one party's approach does not meet the expectations of the other.

The usual starting point in any analysis of expectations is that we all expect to be treated with respect, and with due recognition of our different skills, experiences and perspectives. For instance, we should not talk down to ministers (although some colleagues seem to forget this) or to the public (ditto), and ministers should not talk down to us. Sometimes, however, this approach needs to be abandoned. For instance, you may need to defer to a minister or manager, e.g. if time is short, or if he or she clearly has much more experience or knowledge than you, or if he or she has already heard enough and wants you to accept their decision. The need for you to do so is usually signalled pretty clearly. If you are slow to notice the signals then problems will certainly follow. Equally, excessive use of deference can also cause problems. Ministers, managers and the public expect to deal, most of the time, with experienced, professional civil servants. Lengthy displays of deference will cause them to write you off as inferior in ability as well as status.

So if your relationship with someone seems to be fraught or distant, or if you suspect that they actively dislike you, consider carefully whether you are signalling superiority, equality or inferiority when they are expecting something else. (Psychologists call this transactional analysis.) It is then usually best if you change your approach to meet the expectations of the other, but it might be necessary to signal strongly to the other person that you expect them to adopt a different approach when dealing with you.

Finally, we need to work with people as they really are, not as we would wish them to be. We are each, to different extents, extrovert, introvert, practical, creative, analytical, driven by beliefs, flexible and structured. Some people will be quite different from you, and you will think them decidedly odd. You must put all this on one side when assessing whether the person concerned is talking sense and acting effectively. But you should learn to go further and to some extent adapt your own behaviour to the character of the person with whom you are dealing. If you proudly treat everyone in the same way, you are certainly not dealing effectively with many of them.

MANAGING MEETINGS

It is often remarked, with much truth, that meetings are ever popular as a practical and convivial alternative to work. But busy managers nowadays complain that they attend too many meetings with no clear objectives, no specific length, rambling discussions, no follow-up action and too many people present. The remedies are therefore pretty obvious.

If you will be chairing the meeting, take a minute or two to clarify the purpose of the meeting. What will have been achieved if the meeting has been successful? Also think carefully about who should attend. Attendance should be firmly linked to the purpose of the meeting. If a decision is to be taken, you need to invite only those who need to be committed to the decision. If it is a planning meeting, you need to invite only those who can bring important information and advice to the planning process. You should then make sure that everyone knows the purpose of the meeting, preferably by letting them have a short note in writing. This gives them an opportunity to suggest the names of others who might attend, or to suggest that they need not attend themselves.

If you are invited to a meeting, ensure that you understand the purpose of the meeting, if necessary by talking to the chairman, or to the private secretary in the case of a meeting with a minister. Then consider whether you really need to attend, in order to contribute information or to the discussion. Remember that it is seldom necessary for two people from the same team to attend a meeting that is not central to the objectives of that team. It saves a lot of time if only one person attends and reports the outcome to the other.

Unless there is only one easily defined subject, there should be an agenda, preferably circulated in advance. The chair should decide, at the beginning of the meeting, approximately how much time will be given to each agenda item, and should give this information to those attending. And unless the chair is certain that everyone knows everyone else, all attending should be asked to give their name and division, department etc. In a large pre-orchestrated meeting, it is better to prepare nameplates.

Those introducing papers circulated before the meeting should assume that they have been read, and should therefore limit their comments to emphasising one or two key points, conclusions or recommendations.

A note of the discussion should not be prepared unless it will clearly be helpful either for those who were not at the

meeting, or in order to record discussion, for public accountability reasons, of a particularly difficult issue. However, a
note of action points must always be prepared and circulated
to all present. The chair should appoint someone to do this
(or someone to take a full note if necessary) either before or
at the beginning of the meeting. An electronic white board
is particularly useful, because action points can be written
down as they occur and in full view of everyone, and can
then be printed off and distributed at the end of the meeting.
Otherwise use a flip chart.

It is particularly important that names and timescales are
attached to action points. And progress on all action points
should either be reviewed at a further meeting on the same
subject, or by the chair or their nominee if no further meeting
is to be held within an appropriate timescale.

MANAGING NEGOTIATIONS

We spend much of our time in negotiation – trying to reach
agreement with colleagues or those outside government.
This note provides advice that should be borne in mind if the
negotiations seem likely to be important or difficult.

The first thing you need to do is identify the nature of the
negotiation. Is one party setting out 'to win', not worrying
about the fairness of the outcome? Is one party willing, if necessary, to force through their preferred result? If so, then you
probably need to be familiar with game theory, auction theory

and other strategies. You could do worse than start by reading Thomas Schelling's *The Strategy of Conflict* – as readable, relevant and thought-provoking today as when it was first published back in the 1960s.

Hopefully, however, you will be negotiating with those who want to maintain a satisfactory long-term relationship and to reach a durable agreement that fairly resolves conflicting interests. If so, then read on!

Thorough planning is essential. You need to think carefully about all aspects of the issue, and the likely concerns of the other parties, or you will be surprised and outmanoeuvred at each stage. Make sure in particular that you know all the relevant facts. Make sure, too, that you have a good idea of what drives your minister and how they would react if they were at the negotiating table. Do you know the limits of your negotiating power? In what circumstances do you need to refer back to ministers and/or others in government?

You must establish your minimum and maximum requirements – i.e. the area within which you are free to negotiate. You must decide in advance that, if you do not reach your minimum requirements, you will have to walk away without agreement. Your minimum requirements should therefore be the result of a logical review of the situation in which you find yourself, and should be agreed with those to whom you are reporting. Try to avoid using the phrase 'bottom line'. This means different things to different people, and is often no more than the current limit of your negotiating brief, i.e. the point at which you have to report back to others. If there are no

circumstances in which you can walk away from the negotiation, then you should be clear about this from the beginning.

Take time to examine the issue through the eyes of the
other parties. In particular, what are their likely minimum and
maximum requirements, including non-negotiables? Listen
carefully to what they say during the negotiation. You need to
identify areas of common ground so that you can have a negotiation that maximises the benefit to all the parties.

You should set out to manage the process, ensuring that
all the issues are identified and dealt with in a business-like
way. Keep recording and reviewing what has been agreed so
that there can be no misunderstanding and so that the area
of disagreement is steadily reduced.

Be upfront about non-negotiables but otherwise generally avoid being either 'tough' or 'nice'. The first, if met by
toughness, will only lead to deadlock. The second will lead
to your arriving at an unfair result unless all the other parties
also act nice – which is unlikely. Try to defuse heated argument. The best approach is usually to be sensitive to the other
people, but resolute about the problem. If apparently dead-
locked, consider offering a face-saver (without going below
your minimum requirements). Or be creative. Surprise the
other parties by coming at the issue in a totally different way.

Finally, and this is important, always call a short adjournment when you appear to have reached agreement but before
settling on it. You need to reflect on what you have agreed to
make sure that it is sensible, fair and consistent with your
negotiating brief. You also need to ensure that you have

dealt with all the issues and have not left any uncertainties or ambiguities.

MANAGING OUR OWN TIME

This is an important skill. We have a duty to the taxpayer to work efficiently. And we all need to balance the demands of work, family and friends, as well as find time for ourselves – to get enough sleep, to relax and to pursue our own interests.

So why are we so often poor time managers? Perhaps we recognise that a good time manager can appear lazy, for they only do what they really have to. We are all reluctant to appear lazy, even if this is a natural accompaniment to great efficiency. Nevertheless, it is worth following the rules below.

Concentrate on Your Objectives and Don't Let Others Control Your Time

Do not be too reactive. It is important that you decide how to spend your time, and that you do not organise your time so as to please other people. First, cut out any activity that does not take you nearer to one of your objectives. For instance:

- Consider whether that meeting, lunch or conference is going to help you achieve your objectives. If not, don't go.

- Read what you need to know, not what it's nice to know. Is it really

likely that those papers will contain important new information?
Will reading them take you nearer to one of your objectives?
If not, don't read them.

- Do you get your hard information, such as statistics, direct
  from source? If so, why read endless commentaries on them?
  Take yourself off all those circulation lists.

- Consider whether it is really essential that the minister should speak
  at, or attend, a particular event. Don't forget that you will in due
  course have to find the time to prepare briefing and write a speech.

- Consider whether you really do need to accompany the minister.

Don't hesitate, when under pressure, to take control of your
time by closing your door, borrowing an empty office, or working at home, in order to avoid interruption. Colleagues should
be assured that they can disturb you if it is really necessary,
but otherwise you should tell callers that you are 'a bit tied
up at the moment'.

If you want a brief word with a colleague, go to see them
so that you can bring the conversation to an end when you are
ready, rather than wait for them to leave you. And if you want
the discussion to be a short one, don't sit down!

Don't worry about refusing to go to a meeting that clashes
with an important prior engagement. If the organiser had
thought it vital that you were there, they would have first checked
your availability. There is more of a problem if you want to be

at the meeting, but the organiser does not much care whether or not you are there. You then have to decide which is the most important. But unless the second engagement is clearly more important, it is common courtesy to stick with the first.

If you do organise or attend a meeting, make sure there is a clear agenda, and decide in advance how much time the subject is worth. If the subject is of some interest to you, but not worth more than a few minutes of your time, ask the person chairing the meeting if you can attend for the key part of the discussion, or tell him or her that you have to leave in so many minutes. Or get someone else to attend on your behalf.

Indeed, the solution to many time management problems is to...

Empower Your Colleagues

Empowerment requires a certain amount of courage and patience. Work should generally be done by the most junior colleague who can be expected to do it properly and find it stimulating. The only exceptions are non-repetitive tasks that you can do quickly and easily yourself. It then often takes less time to do it yourself than to tell someone else what needs to be done.

Few of us empower effectively. A significant proportion of what we do could generally be done by colleagues, if we were prepared to invest a little time in training and guidance. This investment of time can seem a burden if you are already under pressure, but the payback can be amazingly quick. You will not only free up your own time; you will also improve the quality of your colleagues' jobs.

So now you are thoroughly lazy, but still have too much to do. You must now improve the way you organise your work.

The essential first step is to...

Prioritise Your Activities

It is in the nature of our work that 80 per cent of our results will come from 20 per cent of activities. It is therefore very helpful to prioritise your work fairly frequently. You should then concentrate on those tasks that are going to be the most effective in getting you closer to your objectives. Leave the lower-priority tasks to later in the day, or tomorrow. By definition, it does not matter if you do not finish them today. You can then go home at a reasonable time, secure in the knowledge that you have done your most effective work.

In prioritising your work, it is useful to decide whether it is (a) urgent and (b) important. If it is both urgent and important, you should do it as soon as possible. If it is urgent but not important, delegate it to someone else. If it is important and not urgent, do it later. If it is neither urgent nor important, don't do it!

Paper Handling

A very good rule is to handle each piece of paper only once. For instance, if you read a letter, and know what you want to say in reply, dictate the reply straight away. Otherwise you will just have to reread the letter, and rethink the reply, on another occasion. Alternatively, delegate the paper to someone else, or throw it in the bin. The only paper that should be put on one side is that which (a) is important, (b) requires considerable thought, and (c) is not urgent.

Finally...

We All Procrastinate

Procrastination is almost always born out of some sort of anxiety. We therefore all need to adopt our own personal solution to this problem. Once you realise that you are putting off a difficult task, you need to plan your campaign accordingly. Set aside a time and place to tackle it. Decide that you will not have lunch, or not go to bed, until you have done so. Spread the papers out. We each can develop our own individual technique. The important thing is to begin the process. You know very well that the task will appear much easier – and less scary – once you have started.

WHOSE PROBLEM IS IT ANYWAY?

This should be the first question you ask when you are faced with a task, problem or issue which seems particularly complex, hard to handle or embarrassing. It is surprising how often a few moments' analysis can lead you to break the problem down into manageable pieces, each to be dealt with by separate people. Indeed, you will often find that the underlying problem does not belong to you, or your minister, in the first place, whereupon you can relax! A few examples might help:

- If you are concerned about the performance of one of your staff then the problem, in the final analysis, is theirs rather than yours. It is for you, not them, to set standards – that is why you have been asked to manage their work. It may be that your colleague can convince you that you have not given them full credit for certain aspects of their work. Or they might tell you about a temporary problem (e.g. health or domestic difficulties) that is affecting their performance. Failing that, they must either change or improve if they are to avoid the consequences of your concern. Of course, the colleague might transfer the problem back to you, e.g. by explaining that they are not clear about their objectives, or persuading you they do not have the right resources. But now you have something to fasten on to and the step-by-step identification of the owner of the problem can lead to its resolution.

- If someone applies for some sort of permission, or financial support, and provides insufficient information, or information which suggests that it should be refused, then again the problem is theirs, not yours. You must be prepared to say 'no' and not wimp out by asking further questions. Of course, you should also explain the nature of the difficulty so that the company or person can decide whether to commit resources to overcoming your objection. But you must make it clear that the decision to do so is theirs, not yours. For goodness sake do not appear to encourage them to do lots of work flexing an application that is almost bound to fail.

- Much the same applies to the person who presses for a quick decision, before you have been able to carry out the necessary consultations or checks. If it is truly impossible to consider the case properly in the time available, you should simply explain that the current decision would be unfavourable. It is for them to decide whether to require you to meet their deadline, or to extend it. (And it is surprising how often they do the latter.)

- And if you are waiting for a task to be completed, or for money or information, the problem is the provider's, not yours. You should get the provider to give you a definite date by which it will appear, beyond which they know that you will hold them responsible for any consequences. The date is then their problem and they can hardly complain if you take unwelcome action after they have failed to meet a deadline that they themselves have set. And it is much better to accept one distant deadline than to be forced into giving frequent extensions.

FINAL COMMENTS

Prime Minister Harold Wilson famously said that a week is a long time in politics. The resultant excitement is of course one of the attractions of working closely with politicians, along with the satisfaction of helping ministers take decisions that will affect so many lives. But unpredictability can be stressful, and ministers can be demanding clients, so it is hard not to feel nervous when providing advice with potentially far-reaching consequences.

It is equally true that a week can be a long time if you are working in a government office, dealing with nervous, anxious or angry members of the public. Providing a good service in that environment is just as difficult as working in Whitehall, as well as being equally rewarding and fulfilling.

Working under pressure can be debilitating if you are inexperienced or ill prepared. I have therefore been enormously grateful to my more experienced colleagues who have provided me with encouragement, advice and training – and forgiven my all too many mistakes. They have embodied the four core civil service values – integrity, honesty, objectivity and impartiality – which together create a great culture in which to work. I have been very glad to follow their example and write this book so as to pass on the benefit of their and my knowledge and experience to the next generation.

Annex A

Ministerial Correspondence

REPLIES TO INVITATIONS

REPLIES TO UNSIGNED invitation cards follow the standard form of words set out below, and neither the minister nor the private secretary signs the reply:

Mr ... thanks the President of the Worshipful Company of Toast Fork Manufacturers for her kind invitation to the reception on ... [and is glad to accept / but regrets that he is unable to attend].

Letters declining invitations to specific events usually start by thanking the correspondent 'for his/her kind invitation to' or 'for kindly inviting me to' the event. There then follows one of a range of possible formulae, depending on the underlying reason for the refusal. Similar formulae can sometimes be used to decline invitations to, say, write magazine articles. But you should always avoid dishonesty. It has a nasty habit of being detected.

Some examples, for ministerial or private secretary signature, are as follows:

Standard refusals

However, as I am sure you will appreciate, the minister receives many requests of this kind and cannot accommodate them all. She therefore regrets that she must decline your invitation on this occasion.

Or:

... but sadly, pressures on her diary are such that she is unable to accept.

Or:

Regretfully I must decline. As you can imagine, I receive many invitations from a number of excellent candidates but cannot, unfortunately, respond positively to them all.

Or:

> As I am sure you will appreciate, I receive many invitations of this kind. I am sorry that I have to decline your invitation on this occasion.

If the invitation is in respect of a particularly busy period

> Unfortunately, due to heavy diary commitments around that time, I am unable to accept your invitation.

Or:

> Unfortunately her diary is particularly full during the period in question and she therefore regrets that she will be unable to accept your invitation.

If there is a definite prior engagement

> Unfortunately I [have a prior engagement / will be abroad at the time] and so must regretfully decline your invitation.

But if you have checked that another minister is willing to take on the engagement and that the substitution is probably acceptable to the hosts, the minister might add:

> However, I understand that [another minister] would be glad to

address the conference. If this would be acceptable, perhaps your secretary could contact his diary secretary (tel: 020 7 …) to confirm the arrangements.

A refusal to have a further meeting with those interested in a familiar subject

Drafted in this case for either prime ministerial or private secretary reply, such a letter might read:

As you know, [ministers] met … on … [and are fully aware of the importance of this subject to your constituents / and they are keeping in close touch with developments.] [I / They] do not therefore think that there would be any practical value in holding an additional meeting.

If appropriate, the letter can be rounded off with best wishes for the success of the event. Examples are:

However, I hope that the dinner is a great success.

Or:

The minister was, however, pleased to note … and has asked me to send you his [congratulations and] good wishes for the future.

Or:

> She would however like to send her best wishes for what she hopes
> will be [a / an interesting and] successful event.

It can be more difficult to decline a general invitation e.g. to visit a company when next in the area. But the minister might use one of the standard refusals above or, if true, simply say:

> I have no plans to visit the area in the near future.

But if the minister means it, he or she might add:

> ... but if I [am / or another minister is] in the area [I will / we shall]
> certainly bear [the company] in mind.

Or a private secretary might add:

> He will certainly keep the company in mind for inclusion in a future
> visit to the area if possible.

(But note that the use of either of these formulae will require the appropriate local office to make an effort to include the company in a future visiting programme.)

Annex B

Policy Making:
World-Class Policy Tests

Y OU CANNOT HAVE good or great policy without placing implementation at the heart of your thinking. That means engaging colleagues in delivery agencies and wider at the very outset of policy development and throughout the process.

Keep thinking about these tests as you work through the policy-making and implementation process. Often you will not be able to pass all of the tests straight away or all of the time. Yes, we have to be realistic about the timescales faced when working with ministers and iterating policy, and pragmatic about policy imperatives affecting a course of action. But that cannot be an excuse for failing to use these tests whenever possible, in how we think about doing our own jobs well, and how we offer challenge and support to colleagues and staff.

1. Purpose: Are you absolutely clear what the government wants to achieve?

2. Role: Are you absolutely clear what the government's role is?

3. Evidence: Are you confident that you are providing world-leading policy advice based on the very latest expert thinking, data and analysis?

4. Creativity: Are you confident that you have explored the most radical and creative ideas available in this policy space ... including doing nothing?

5. Delivery: Are you confident that your preferred approach can be delivered, and in the timescales proposed?

In more detail:

1. What's the point?

Purpose: Are you absolutely clear what the government wants to achieve?

- Do you have a very clear picture of the high-level outcomes and outputs that the government would like to see?

- Can you describe what the market or service or system would look like if it were functioning properly to deliver the outcomes needed?

- Do you have a clear sense of how it would feel for those receiving the services, whoever they are, if the outcomes were achieved?

- Would they recognise your description?

- Have you described this to ministers and checked your understanding is correct?

If your job is managing or implementing policy, are you absolutely clear what the policy you're implementing is meant to achieve and how/why?

If not, find out or you might be pushing things in the wrong direction.

2. What's it got to do with us?

Role: Are you absolutely clear what the government's role is?

- Is there definitely a problem here that can only be solved through some kind of government intervention? Really? Are you absolutely sure?

- Are you about to nationalise a problem that should be dealt with elsewhere?

- Is it a problem that has actually manifested itself and cannot be resolved through other people? What's your evidence for that?

- Was your starting point that we trust expert practitioners and professionals on the front line to know what is best?

- Would you feel comfortable setting out how your policy advice fits in with the government's wider agenda? If ministers want to reduce the role of government and deregulate, for instance, how could you justify new activity and legislation?

- Can you be confident that you are not about to make the problem worse or create a new problem through your policy advice – no matter how well intentioned?

- Will you actually be able to demonstrate whether or not your policy has made a positive or negative impact?

- Have you considered how that impact might be different for different groups of people?

If your job is managing or implementing policy, how confident are you that what you're doing couldn't be done by someone else if you stopped doing it; or couldn't be done better in a different way; or that you're not making things worse; and how do you actually know?

3. Who made you the expert?

Evidence: Are you confident that you are providing world-leading policy advice based on the very latest expert thinking?

- Who is the world's leading expert in this policy area?

- Have you consulted them on their work?

- Have you delved into the archives to see how we tackled this problem last time (or when something similar arose)?

- Could you, if asked, produce a bibliography of evidence for your policy submission? Would it look impressive and balanced or thin and one-sided?

- Have you consulted with specialist analysts who know most about the area?

- Have you deployed clear economic and behavioural analysis on the problem?

- Have you got a robust value-for-money case for suggesting any spending – and are you trying to spend as little taxpayer money as possible on fixing the problem?

If your job is managing or implementing policy, is your experience of implementation suggesting new evidence on how the policy could be improved or do you think it is perfect? Are you deliberately getting feedback on the quality of the policy and/or the quality of implementation from different groups of customers/stakeholders – and is this feeding back into policy and implementation design? Have you explored world-leading delivery organisations and how they would implement a policy like this?

4. Is your advice predictable?

Creativity: Are you confident that you have explored the most radical and creative ideas available in this policy space ... including doing nothing?

- Do you feel confident that stakeholders or ministers or anyone else will be unable to come up with an idea you haven't thought of?

- Will ministers be pleasantly surprised by your creative thinking?

- Have you looked at evidence from other fields and policy areas addressing similar questions?

- Have you had an open process of generating ideas?

- Have you shied away from any idea because you thought it was too radical? If so, why?

- Have you come up with something that is very deliverable but won't actually solve the problem you're trying to solve?

- Have you set boundaries around your creative process like 'stakeholders won't like it'? And if so, what happens if you take them off and think about what new options are available?

If your job is managing or implementing policy, are you constantly thinking about how the process could be improved and putting ideas forward? Or are you just turning the handle on the machine without thinking too hard about how the machine could be re-engineered?

5. But will it actually work?

Delivery: Are you confident that your preferred approach can be delivered?

- Have you worked closely with colleagues in the relevant delivery agencies at every stage of developing your policy solution?

- Are you confident that you have considered the delivery implications and risks in your preferred policy approach?

- Are you clear on the costs through the system and life of the policy?

- Have you thought about the burdens it will put into the system – including the administrative burdens?

- Have you created something that is as simple as it can be?

- Have you listened to experts on the ground and stakeholders, but done so in a challenging way to determine what legitimate concerns are and what is undue caution or resistance to radical ideas?

- Are you confident you have designed something that can easily be used by service users and the general public, rather than designed for the approval of experts in the sector?

If your job is managing and implementing policy, have you recognised that you have a responsibility to find out if the policy you are busily implementing is actually working for all the people and groups that you serve and is being implemented fully? If not, why not? How can it be improved? Is there a flaw in the policy that means it can't be implemented and which needs to be fed back up the line?

And then ...

If you pass these tests, ask:

- Would I be comfortable exposing my policy thinking to the most challenging minds around? If not, it probably needs more work. If yes, go and do it but invite challenge to help you test your thinking and improve the final product.

- Is my policy advice logically and crisply argued and free of jargon? Have you drafted your way through difficult issues and fudged them rather than working out exactly what you think and explaining that? If somebody wanted to criticise your ideas, what would their arguments be? And what would be your response to those arguments? Have you explained the essential issue and advice in a few pages, so that it can be understood quickly by someone with minimal understanding of the subject area and a full box of work?

- Is it free from errors? If you were to be fined £5 for every typo, spelling error, arithmetical or other mistake in your submission, would you be comfortable hitting the 'Send' button now? If not, print it off and sit in a quiet room to read it through, or ask someone else to; don't expect ministers or senior officials or private offices to spot and correct your mistakes.

- Will my analysis and thinking be available for others to use and learn from? Are you making sure that your work, knowledge and contacts can be accessed by the next person who runs your policy or by someone elsewhere in the department or government who needs to understand and learn from you?

Source: Department for Education policy assessment document, with minor adjustments to make it of general application.

Annex C

Recruitment: Some Possible Lines of Questioning

MANY CIVIL SERVICE job advertisements require candidates to be good team-workers, have good communication and interpersonal skills etc. etc. But what does this mean in practice? The late Nancy Holloway offered the following definitions, which others might find both helpful and thought-provoking.

Teamwork/flexibility

- Are you a friendly and approachable colleague and will you get on with the team you are in and the wider culture, including working with other teams without any problem, and freely sharing information?

- Will you be happy to have new bits of work thrown at you/work to a different boss from time to time/work in project management style in different teams with people from around the office?

Communication/interpersonal skills

- Can you write well?

- Can you speak coherently and (for more senior posts) compellingly when briefing or presenting information?

- Can you organise your thoughts and present them in a concise manner/get your message across in plain English?

- Do you relate well to other humans (as opposed to machines etc.) and are you able to strike the right note with external stakeholders in meetings/phone calls etc.?

- Can you read others well, and respond appropriately?

Management/organisational skills

- Can you manage other people without either diving in too deeply and doing their work for them or leaving them without guidance?

- Are you selfish about claiming credit or can you coach and help others develop?

- Can you work in a no-blame culture but still get people to perform?

- Can you organise your own work/work to deadlines?

- Can you juggle conflicting priorities?

- Can you use IT well and manage paperwork?

Analytical skills/ability to deal with complex information and data/solution-focused

- Are you able to stand back from an issue, pick out important issues in problems you're dealing with, find solutions/ ways forward?

- Are you able to relate your issues both to those within the office you are dealing with and to the bigger picture for the organisation as a whole, including corporate aims and objectives?

- Are you able to sift through large quantities of information or data and quickly see problem areas?

- Are you able to present a coherent and well-argued solution/ way forward?

Self-starter/ability to work on own initiative/multi-tasker

- Are you the sort of person who doesn't sit and wait for someone to tell you what to do, has ideas, is quick to learn, makes suggestions for improvements, and gets on with work on your own without constant supervision and advice?

- Are you able to think on your feet and respond to changing situations?

- Are you able to juggle a number of things at once and be able to work out which is most important/urgent?

- Do you know when to ask for help and from whom?

Representational skills (if appropriate)

- Will you be able to represent the organisation in public fora or at meetings with stakeholders?

- Will you be able to demonstrate an understanding of issues around the office and an ability to relate them coherently to others?

- Are you able to hold your own when briefing senior people?

Regulatory aptitude (if appropriate)

- Are you comfortable with both collaborating and confronting people/issues with external stakeholders, and do you know when to choose the correct one of these approaches?

- Do you feel comfortable with economic concepts and working with economists?

- Do you feel comfortable working within a legal framework which controls the limits of what you can do, and working with lawyers?

- Can you see around corners and anticipate trouble before it happens?

- Do you have a questioning mind that doesn't just accept things you're told at face value?

- Can you negotiate with difficult people?

Annex D

Project Management: A Detailed Checklist

1. Determine the scope: what to deliver and when.

   - Describe why the work needs to be done – for example, to meet a policy imperative or respond to a business driver for change.

   - Describe the required outcome in measurable, time-based terms – what you want to change and how you will know that you have changed it.

   - Identify high-level benefits, how they contribute to strategic objectives and how they will be measured. Identify the causal factors – what needs to be in place for the outcome to happen?

- Describe the actions/projects that need to be undertaken.

- Identify high-level options for meeting the business need; identify the option with the most acceptable mix of cost, benefit and risk.

2. Estimate the resources and capabilities (people, physical resources and funding) you will need.

- Base your estimates on what others have done, wherever possible.

- Look at the dependencies between current programmes and projects in your organisation to arrive at the optimum allocation of resources. Establish the skills and expertise you need (capability to do the job) and the numbers of people who will be required over the lifetime of the project (capacity).

- Estimate the whole-life cost of the change – people and physical resources (buildings, technology etc.).

- Consider whether your organisation has enough experience and skills to manage new arrangements where they involve working with others.

- Determine the budget/resource limits and where the costs will fall.

3. Identify potential sources of capability.

   • Investigate who could deliver the required outcome. Look at
     the whole supply chain – your organisation, business partners,
     suppliers and their suppliers, your advisers and your customers.

   • Consider innovative ways of delivery, such as collaborating
     with the private sector where there are appropriate incentives
     for them to do so.

   • Look at what others are doing.

   • Where relevant, look at opportunities to exploit technology
     to deliver the capability you need.

4. Decide who will carry out the required processes and policies.

   • Look at the proposed way(s) forward in the context of the
     business, its current portfolio and priorities; check that they
     fit with the organisation's strategy.

   • Check for opportunities to collaborate with others and for
     overlaps with projects already planned or underway; look at
     the interfaces with other initiatives/organisations.

   • Establish how much is new or changing in terms of people
     and the way they work, services and physical resources such as
     buildings and IT. Make a realistic assessment of the likelihood

of success, given your organisation's existing commitments, priorities, capability and capacity.

- Consider whether critical business processes would be affected.

- Consider breaking the work down into smaller packages instead of doing everything at once.

- Revisit the priorities; in addition, expect the unexpected – could you cope with unforeseen change?

5. Determine who will be accountable for what.

- Establish who will be responsible for making investment decisions (for example, the board, partners) and who will be the senior individual responsible for the project/programme as its owner.

- Check that the right person is given the role, in terms of their authority and responsibilities in relation to the proposed change.

- Define high-level governance structures and responsibilities; consider how different responsibilities fit together and how everyone involved will understand their role and responsibility.

- Define high-level arrangements for reporting downwards on policy and business requirements, reporting upwards on progress, performance and risks and taking prompt action as required.

- For joint projects, identify the additional arrangements that need to be in place.

- Ensure that reporting lines will be kept as short as possible.

6. Identify similar projects that have succeeded.

    - Compare your project with other ways of delivering a similar outcome – public/private sector and internationally.

    - Take account of factors that could affect success, such as cultural differences.

    - Identify why others have succeeded – or failed – and the lessons learned from their experiences.

7. Determine an acceptable balance of cost, benefit and risk – and how they should be managed.

    - Confirm the solution that offers best value for money; obtain approval from senior management.

    - Revisit the key risks to performance and delivery. Risks relating to performance could include lack of public interest leading to poor take-up of a service; risks relating to delivery could include overambitious timescales, inadequate resources and lack of essential skills.

- Consider the whole supply chain, including intermediaries, and how risks could be allocated and managed.

- For the proposed way forward, identify an acceptable balance of costs, benefits and risk.

- Consider a wide range of possibilities and the trade-offs associated with each.

- If it is an innovative approach, consider how to manage the risks and how well your organisation could cope with the scale of change proposed by more radical options.

- Establish that each of the proposed options is practical, realistic and viable; consider how well each option meets stakeholder needs.

- Contingency plans need to be outlined at this stage.

8. Determine how you will work with other delivery agents and stakeholders to share information and knowledge.

- Consider who your stakeholders are and what they want – that is, the people who will be involved in/affected by the change and/or influence the outcome.

- Resolve any conflicting demands.

- Think about how you will achieve stakeholder buy-in and overcome any resistance to the change.

- Consider the perceptions that might have to change and how behaviours could be changed.

9. Determine arrangements for monitoring and reporting progress. Identify the performance measures and incentives you will need.

- Set milestones – that is, progress checkpoints at specified intervals – against intermediate targets towards the required outcome. These milestones will enable you to track progress against plans and take action on any feedback relating to progress.

- Identify performance measures that are SMART (specific, measurable, achievable, realistic and time-based); determine mechanisms for reliable and regular performance information.

- Think about the incentives for staff, partners and suppliers that will encourage a successful outcome.

- Check that performance information can be collected efficiently and in good time to take remedial action if required.

Acknowledgements and Further Reading

MOST IF NOT all of the advice in this book was originally provided by my many civil service colleagues, not least in the four departments in which I served. They are of course too numerous to mention, but I owe them a great debt of gratitude. I do, however, want to say a special thank-you to four colleagues who have made a particular contribution to this third edition. Christopher Jary and David Laughrin offered many perceptive suggestions and comments on my working draft; Susannah Simon was very helpful in updating the advice on working effectively within the European Union; and Richard Cooke's comments were equally valuable in reminding me of the surprisingly many changes that have been made to parliamentary procedures since I last sat in the officials' box.

This prompts me to acknowledge that the UK civil service is undergoing a period of profound change, so some of the advice in this book will need to be corrected and updated. I will publish such revised advice on the accompanying website, www.civilservant.org.uk. This website also includes an online library and recommended further reading, as well as much more detailed information about civil service reform, special advisers, ministerial directions and so on. I would, however, draw particular attention to David Laughrin's 'In Their Own Words: What Ministers Think of Civil Service Support', which provided many of the quotations in this book, and to John Hutton and Leigh Lewis's How to Be a Minister, which provides very readable additional advice to many of the themes in this book.

I recognise that the guidance in this book does not directly deal with the particular challenges facing the vast majority of civil servants who work in executive agencies and local offices. Neither does it deal with the particular circumstances of those working in the devolved administrations. I apologise to such colleagues but I hope that they too will find the majority of the text to be helpful, whilst the Whitehall-centric sections will tell them something about the working methods of those whose decisions have such a major influence on their working lives.

Finally, I offer sincere thanks to Iain Dale who, many years ago now, encouraged me to write the first two editions of this book, and has since chivvied me into writing this subsequent version – and to his editor, Olivia Beattie, who cheerfully and expertly knocked this third edition into publishable state.